THE POLITICS OF ILLUSION

THE
POLITICS
OF ILLUSION
THE FISCHER CONTROVERSY IN GERMAN HISTORIOGRAPHY

JOHN A. MOSES
Reader in History
University of Queensland

BARNES & NOBLE
BOOKS
10 East 53d St., New York 10022
(a division of Harper & Row Publishers, Inc.)

First published in 1975 by
George Prior Publishers,
Rugby Chambers, 2 Rugby Street,
London, WC1, England

Published in the U.S.A. 1975 by
Harper & Row Publishers, Inc.
Barnes & Noble Import Division

ISBN 0-06-495000-X

Printed in England by
Burgess & Son (Abingdon) Ltd.,
Abingdon, Oxfordshire

DEN ERLANGER LEHRERN

CONTENTS

FOREWORD

I am happy to commend Dr. Moses' study of German historians and their influence on the politics of their country. English-speaking students will find here an excellent analysis of the issues, not just about the origins of the first world war, but about the wider questions of the responsibility of historians in general. In the cataclysms of this century, Germany has played a decisive role. Today there are two Germanies, each standing for divergent ideologies. In each, the historians have challenged the received notions of their predecessors, and a vigorous debate has ensued about the continuity or otherwise in the policies of Germany's rulers, particularly in the seventy-five turbulent years between 1870 and 1945.

Dr. Moses' able elucidation of the work and influence of Professor Fritz Fischer demonstrates how, in West Germany, the campaign has been fought to attack the assumption that the historians' principal task is to provide ideological justifications of national policy. We are all in debt to Fischer for his scholarly revision of the long-held view that Germany was not responsible for the outbreak of the war in 1914, or the equally seductive view that she was no more responsible than others. We are also in debt to Fischer and his school for the growth of a pluralistic view of Germany's history, which is as ready to condemn as to praise those policies and personalities which were so long regarded as sacrosanct.

This lucid account of the debate still continuing in Germany is a valuable guide, which will undoubtedly lead students of German history, and indeed historians generally, to re-examine their presuppositions about the historians' role in society and the influence they carry in determining the nations' policies. The task of the historian, Fischer claims, is to exercise a critical vigilance over trends within his own as well as other countries. If this principle is now being heeded in West Germany, it is equally applicable elsewhere. We are grateful to John Moses for his stimulating survey of this important discussion.

JOHN S. CONWAY
Professor
Department of History
University of British Columbia

April 1975

Author's Preface

The dramatic revolution in German historiography, which was begun by Fritz Fischer in 1961 with the publication of his *Griff nach der Weltmacht* (English translation: *Germany's Aims in the First World War*) and which unleashed a bitter debate among German historians, experienced a second phase with the publication by Fischer in 1969 of *Krieg der Illusionen* (English translation: *War of Illusions*, 1974). This entire argument has been the most graphic revelation for western observers. It is now possible to see more clearly than ever before what a central, and in the event, disastrous political-pedagogic role the academic historian used to play in Germany before 1945. It had, of course, been long suspected, as Herbert Butterfield pointed out in 1954, that German historical scholarship had had anything but a salutary effect on the political consciousness of the German people.[1] The few courageous liberally-minded German scholars of the nineteen-twenties and 'thirties who had protested against excessive nationalism in historical writing[2] did not have sufficient time to make an impact on the historical scholarship of their homeland because they either died too early or had to emigrate with the advent of the Third Reich. Those who remained in Germany were effectively silenced.

After 1945 which was regarded by many German scholars as *das Jahr null*, the year nought, when a totally fresh start had to be made, when everything had to be reconstructed, including the writing of the nation's history, there began to

[1] Herbert Butterfield, *Man on His Past*, pp. 26–27.
[2] George W. F. Hallgarten, *Das Schicksal des Imperialismus im 20. Jahrhundert*, pp. 70–89. The writers referred to here were Eckart Kehr, Friedrich Wilhelm Foerster, Veit Valentin and Karl Kautsky.

appear books and articles which stressed the need for a radical revision of the German historical discipline. Both conservative and liberal historians were pondering in particular the contribution of their discipline to the intellectual climate out of which National Socialism could emerge. There was a genuine seeking after new perspectives in trying to arrive at a satisfactory explanation for this development. Although many of these pointed to the strong national tradition in German historiography, none of them succeeded as it were in stirring up the "guild" (i.e. the university professors of history) to make a really radical revision or repudiation of the dominant tradition in German historiography.[3] It remained for the prominent Hamburg historian, Fritz Fischer, himself deeply rooted in that tradition, to pick up the torch which had been ignited first in the Weimar epoch, and pioneer a veritable intellectual revolution in his profession. That is to say, Fritz Fischer after 1945 courageously began to rewrite German history as a militant liberal[4] and not as an apologist or propagandist for national "honour". Because he has done this with so much success, Fischer has been angrily

[3] It would certainly be an injustice to omit reference to a number of German scholars, who after 1945 in a spirit of frank self-examination, began to put forward new assessments about the assumptions upon which history was written and taught in Germany. Some of these are represented in Hans Kohn's useful collection of essays, *German History, Some New German Views* (London, 1954). Also relevant here is my paper, "The Crisis in West German Historiography: Origins and Trends", *HS* XIII (1969), in which the major revisionists are identified. None of these, however, went so far as to ignite a revolution in German historical thought though some liberals such as Franz Schnabel had always adopted an anti-nationalist stance. The credit for the present revolutionary trend, i.e. a movement which swept the entire profession along with it, must surely go to Fritz Fischer. The first definite signs of his repudiation of the statist tradition can be seen in the paper he delivered at the Munich conference of German historians in 1949, "Der deutsche Protestantismus und die Politik im 19. Jahrhundert". *HZ* CLXXI (1951). It is puzzling why Professor Kohn omitted this paper from his otherwise valuable symposium.

[4] Wolfgang Beutin, "Fritz Fischer oder wurde der erste Weltkrieg inszeniert?" in *Wer lehrt an deutschen Universitäten?* ed. Karlheinz Deschner, pp. 135–6.

accused by at least one of his older colleagues of having betrayed his country (*Landesverrat*).

This is a situation which merits our attention, not only because as students of modern history we are obliged to keep abreast of new trends in research but also because we have here an outstanding example of the political function of historiography.

Prior to 1945 German historians, with a few notable exceptions, were practising a doctrine known as *Etatismus* or statism in their writing. More than regarding the state as the unit of historical enquiry this meant that they glorified the state where they could and defended it at the cost of truth if they felt they had to. Their values were entirely state-orientated. Now Fischer and his "school", led chiefly by Professor Imanuel Geiss, have done more than any other of the post-war liberal historians to destroy that tradition. In doing so they have come close to being ostracised by their more conservative and traditional colleagues.

Fischer's defiantly liberal approach to the history of German policy before and during the First World War, coupled with the thesis that Hitler's Germany in many central respects merely continued those earlier aggressive policies, have incensed many tradition-minded Germans. Some have reacted with bitter and emotional counter-attacks but the vast majority of academic historians, because they see that Fischer's "bold" theses are so well documented, have maintained a truculent silence or, if they have ventured to duel with Fischer, they have done so in a highly defensive spirit.[5] It will, understandably, take time for the older generation to digest these unpalatable facts.

The Fischer-Geiss research has also much relevance for non-German students of history mainly because of what the debate has revealed about the uses to which "history" can be put. In order to introduce students to this important work a report on the first wave of reaction to the Fischer thesis was published by the present author in 1968 under the title, *The War Aims of*

[5] c.f. Wolfgang Schieder, ed., *Erster Weltkrieg: Ursachen und Kriegsziele*, pp. 11–23.

Imperial Germany: Professor Fritz Fischer and his Critics. This
now needs to be complemented with a more detailed assessment of the overall significance of the "Fischer revolution" and
of the content of the "second book", *Krieg der Illusionen.*

As a student in Germany, the present writer was privileged
to work under scholars of immense erudition, great humanity
and scrupulous integrity. He is aware of his indebtedness to
the late Franz Schnabel who was still teaching in Munich in
1961 and 1962, and particularly to the late Waldemar Besson,
Walther Peter Fuchs and Karl-Heinz Ruffman (all professors
in Erlangen 1963–65). In them the admirable drive for scholarly
objectivity, which is part at least of the timeless legacy of
Leopold von Ranke to all historians, was dominant. Their own
work in its various spheres is eloquent testimony to this. However, it fell to Professor Fritz Fischer in Hamburg to complete
the transformation in historical-political thinking in Germany
which others, like the scholars just mentioned, had been subtly
adumbrating in their lectures and writings in the more recent
post-war period.

Since visiting the History Department in Hamburg briefly
during the Winter Semester 1969/70, and again in 1972, the
present writer has had the opportunity of observing at first hand
the nature and ramifications of the second phase of the "Fischer
controversy". Fischer himself is highly conscious of the fact
that his research is unpopular in many quarters. The same can
be said of Professor Imanuel Geiss and his contribution, but
both scholars are unswerving in their dedication to historical
truth as opposed to national apologetics. It is indeed a cause
for rejoicing that they can continue to put forward unpopular
views and survive academically; in a totalitarian state, historical
research which does not conform to the ruling party line is ruthlessly suppressed. In a very real sense, then, the Fischer controversy has been a commentary on the state of democracy in
the Federal Republic of Germany.

This last point is added reason for taking cognizance of the
debate. Historiography is without doubt related to national
politics. Indeed, the historiography of a particular country is

a sensitive barometer to the political pressures within that country. If the historiography is nationalist in tone, it is surely a sign that the country in question is experiencing a phase of self-adulation and/or self-justification. And because history-writing is not only a reflector but also a moulder of national sentiment, it is by no means politically innocuous. There is a reciprocal action between national politics and national historio-graphy wherein the historian by sustaining past epochs of national glory in the memory of the present contributes to enlivening current national politics. Nationalistic historical writing must ultimately have an effect on the political conscious-ness and will of the population, not to mention on the decision-making statesmen. If, on the other hand, the historiography of a country is a mixture of competing schools where the nationa-lists are openly opposed by the debunkers of false images and sentiment, then it can be claimed that there exists in that country a healthy intellectual and political climate. In such a situation it is difficult for extreme nationalists to gain a mono-poly over the means of influencing the political awareness of the community, especially the school pupils and and university students.

In the Federal Republic of Germany the professional his-torians have for some time since 1945 been at work trying to re-assess historical developments which brought catastrophe to their land. Because there had been a number of serious accounts put forward and because particular German historians had been anxious to enter a dialogue with their European counterparts to eliminate national prejudice from schoolbooks, the intellectual climate was beginning to take on the characteristics of that in any liberal society.[6] There has been a frank and open dis-cussion between those of more traditional concepts and a variety

[6] At this point, too, attention ought to be drawn to the work of that circle of historians concerned with eradicating nationalistic prejudices from school text books. These people were mobilised to a large extent by the late Professor George Eckert who founded the *Schulbuch Institut* in Braunschweig. The history of this establishment which was founded in 1950 is provided by Helmut Hirsch, *Lehrer machen Geschichte* (Wuppertal, 1971).

of revisionists from both the older and post-war generation of scholars. Fritz Fischer's work belongs in this revisionist stream because in a real sense it merely continues what the older Ludwig Dehio began in the early nineteen-fifties with his series of revisionist essays published in English as *Germany and World Politics in the Twentieth Century.* However, Fischer, by going into much greater detail on the origins and course of the First World War has achieved a virtually revolutionary impact not only because he has approached the war-guilt question with ruthless honesty but also has ventured to call into question many of the cherished values and institutions of Wilhelmine Germany, in particular the assumptions of the then dominant school of historians and their political influence. This more than other post-1945 revisionism has caused the unprecedented furore in German academic circles.

Naturally, in such voluminous examples of research as Fischer's work there will be peripheral issues which need further attention. However, one thing stands firm: Fischer has smashed a broad path through the entangled forest of German academic historiography and has pioneered many new avenues for research which are now being investigated. In the course of this process some of them are being approached for the first time or are being re-opened, often with fruitful results. Thereby many a long-established illusion has had to be discarded. The function of historiography now is not to infuse people with enthusiasm for their nation's saga but to achieve a sober understanding of the forces which shaped the present so that the future might be faced with a higher degree of confidence about the durability of rationally-based socio-political order, both national and international. What is, however, a salutary lesson to the outside observer is the realisation that the cherished illusions he most likely has about his own country may also turn out on closer scrutiny to be historical distortions fed to an unsuspecting people by "patriotic" writers and teachers of history. The truth is, indeed, very hard to get at beneath the camouflage of propaganda cleverly put forward in the guise of scholarship. History is therefore a dangerous subject both for the writers and those whom they try to influence. Always it demands the highest degree of critical understanding, honest scepticism and commitment to human, as distinct from exclusively national values.

I wish here to express my indebtedness to those who have contributed to the production of this book. My colleague, Dr. Joseph Siracusa, an authority on the so-called New Left Historiography in the United States, offered much stimulating comment about the political-pedagogic function of historiography in general. Further, Imanuel Geiss, John Röhl, Volker Berghahn, Lothar Kettenacker, Hartmut Pogge von Strandmann, Paul Kennedy, Walter Grab and, above all, Georg Iggers encouraged me in their various ways to complete this survey. Mr. John Robertson rendered invaluable assistance in the final preparation of the manuscript. I should also like to acknowledge the financial assistance provided by the University of Queensland Research Committee. Lastly, I would also like to record my sincere thanks to Mr. Lalit Adolphus, from whose years of editorial experience I have greatly benefited.

J.M.
Brisbane
February 1975.

Abbreviations

AHR ......American Historical Review
AJPH ......Australian Journal of Politics and History
APZ ......Aus Politik und Zeitgeschichte
ASMZ......Allgemeine Schweizerische Militär-Zeitschrift
BIHR ......Bulletin of the Institute of Historical Research
CEH ......Central European History
EA ....Europa Archiv
FH ....Frankfurter Hefte
GWU ......Geschichte in Wissenschaft und Unterricht
HJ ....Historical Journal
HS ....Historical Studies
HZ ....Historische Zeitschrift
JIDG ......Jahrbuch des Instituts für deutsche Geschichte
JES ....Journal of European Studies
KUER......Kyoto University Economic Review
MGM ......Militärgeschichtliche Mitteilungen
NPL ......Neue Politische Literatur
PVS.........Politische Vierteljahresschrift
PWA ......Polish Western Affairs
R d'A......Revue d'Allemagne
SR ....Social Research
TH ....The Historian
UNHJ......The University of Newcastle Historical Journal
           (Australia)
VSWG......Vierteljahresschrift für Sozial — und
           Wirtschaftsgeschichte
VZ ....Vierteljahrshefte für Zeitgeschichte
WH ....Werkhefte — Zeitschrift für Probleme der
           Gesellschaft
ZfG ....Zeitschrift für Geschichtswissenschaft
ZP ....Zeitschrift für Politik

PART ONE

Introduction

As stated in the preface, the author's intention is to convey something of the significance of the "Fischer revolution" in German historiography. In trying to assess the broader significance of what has taken place in German historiography it would, of course, be necessary to analyse the dominating trends from the early nineteenth century up to the present. However, this task has already been accomplished in masterly fashion by Professor Georg Iggers of the State University of New York at Buffalo in his work, *The German Conception of History.* Iggers has taken full cognizance of Fischer's pioneering work, and it is unnecessary to repeat here what has already been so clearly presented. This essay takes an entirely different approach to the problem and was suggested by a number of shorter studies by scholars of differing backgrounds but with the same general field of interest, viz. the interrelationship between historiography and politics. This is surely one of the most fruitful questions to emerge from the entire "Fischer controversy".

In his "first" book Fischer drew attention to the major role played by German historians before 1914 in preparing an intellectual climate favourable to national expansion. In fact, historians were in the vanguard of those writers in Germany who preached the need for increased armament, more colonies and a "place in the sun" for the German fatherland. These writers not only dominated public opinion with their ideas, but were close to the decision-making statesmen who also imbibed them.

In the controversy unleashed by Fischer many contributors have wittingly and unwittingly strengthened one of his main contentions, namely that educated society in Germany in 1914 was eager for war, that many pressure groups worked on the government to pursue certain aims and that this government was so responsive to these ideas and aims that it could not — even if it deemed them imprudent — go against them.

Because of this there has been, understandably, much comment about the motives and concepts of the man at the centre of the power élite, the Imperial Chancellor Bethmann Hollweg. For several reasons this has posed difficulties for the historian. First, no minutes of high-level government meetings were kept in Imperial Germany; and second, Bethmann Hollweg's own personal papers have been destroyed.[7] However, the diary of his private secretary Kurt Riezler has been preserved and this document records the conversations of Bethmann and his confidant during the July–August crisis of 1914. The significance of such a source cannot be overestimated.

In 1964 Professor Karl Dietrich Erdmann of Kiel published a paper in which he presented an evaluation of the Riezler diary as a guide to understanding Bethmann Hollweg's motives during the great crisis. Erdmann's aim was clearly to diminish the stigma of "guilt" on the Chancellor which has been read into Fischer's interpretation.[8] However, Fischer's assistant at that time, Imanuel Geiss, countered Erdmann's paper with a more damaging assessment of the revelations of the Riezler diary and pointed out certain embarrassingly aggressive traits in Riezler's thought as contained in two of his immediate pre-war books on world politics. Geiss had suggested that Riezler's conception of international politics which the Chancellor obviously shared was dangerously irrational.[9]

Subsequent to this, another German historian, Andreas Hillgruber, rallied to the side of Professor Erdmann by presenting an analysis of the July crisis in which he sought to interpret

---

[7] Fritz Stern, "Bethmann Hollweg and the War", in *The Responsibility of Power*, eds. Leonard Krieger and Fritz Stern, p. 254.

[8] Karl Dietrich Erdmann, "Zur Beurteilung Bethmann Hollwegs", *Geschichte in Wissenschaft und Unterricht* XV (1964).

[9] Imanuel Geiss and Hartmut Pogge von Strandmann, *Die Erforderlichkeit des Unmöglichen*, pp. 49–75.

the Chancellor's motives from the ideas which Riezler expressed
in his above-mentioned works together with the revelations of
the diary.[10] What Hillgruber shows most convincingly is that
both Riezler and Bethmann shared a world of ideas with an
understanding of world politics which was obviously derived
from the teaching of the dominant school of historians in
Germany. Hillgruber's aim in showing how Bethmann calculated for war was not by any means to criticise the Chancellor
but rather to show that, given his *Weltanschauung* and his
sense of responsibility to Germany, he could not be expected
to have acted otherwise. In short, having recognised that war
was unavoidable, Bethmann was forced to take the initiative
in the crisis because this was the only way in which he saw
any chance of saving the fatherland from the impending
disaster. His action may have appeared on the surface to have
been aggressive, but the real motive was defensive. These ideas
need ventilating. If Bethmann and Riezler shared the same
ideas on *Weltpolitik* as the dominating historical school, then
this school played, indeed, a fateful role in educating the
German power élite.

It is the aim of the first part of this essay, then, to compare
the ideas of the so-called Neo-Rankean school with those of
Kurt Riezler (and Bethmann Hollweg) with the intention of
illustrating the unique political-pedagogic role exercised by
German historiography prior to the First World War. The historians saw themselves as the "heralds of policy" and were in
this respect highly successful. However, that which they prized

[10] Andreas Hillgruber, "Riezlers Theorie des kalkulierten Risikos und
Bethmann Hollwegs politische Konzeption in der Julikrise 1914",
Historische Zeitschrift CCII (1966). The literature on Bethmann Hollweg
has been rapidly extended in recent years. Already in 1957 Hans-Günter
Zmarzlik, formerly a student of the late Gerhard Ritter, published
Bethmann Hollweg als Reichskanzler 1909–1914 which sought to examine the domestic political entanglement with which the Chancellor
had to contend. A biography by Eberhard von Vietsch appeared in 1969
and an English language study by Konrad Jarausch, *The Enigmatic
Chancellor*, was published in 1973. See also Klaus Hildebrand's short
but very valuable survey of the existing research on the Chancellor
entitled, *Bethmann Hollweg, Der Kanzler ohne Eigenschaften?*

the most, viz. their new fatherland, they inadvertently helped to destroy by propagating a doctrine of international politics which demanded that the state must expand. Their ideological-political influence was a fateful one. It is by underlining this fact and by contrasting (by implication) the aims of the Neo-Rankean historiography with those of the Fischer school today that the significance of the Fischer revolution can be seen.

Part two concerns itself chiefly with tracing the course of the "Fischer controversy" since the publication of the "second" book in 1969 and attempts an evaluation of the impact of the Fischer revolution on the character of present-day West German historiography.

"For in Germany—and indeed all over the Continent—it is by no means considered sufficient that an historical work should tell the truth in accordance with the convictions of the author. In a work dealing with higher policy it is held to go without saying that the author shall enter upon his investigations in the interests of his own nation and against its antagonists, and that his work shall be 'patriotic', and the outcome of 'national feeling'."

HERMANN KANTOROWICZ,
The Spirit of British Policy and the Myth of the Encirclement of Germany, (1929), p. 21

CHAPTER I

Neo-Rankeanism — Ideology of *Weltpolitik*

The history of German historiography is a part of
general German history. It is not a history in itself
but rather touches general and social interrelationships
at every point.[1]

ECKART KEHR (1902–1933)

The author of the above quotation reflecting shortly before the
Nazi seizure of power in Germany on the socio-political function
of German historiography during the nineteenth and twentieth
centuries was drawing attention to the underlying assumption
and tendencies of the work of the academic historians of
his country. Because these professors were in fact economically
dependent upon the state in whose universities they served,
they all tended to support the socio-political *status quo*. Particularly during the Bismarckian-Wilhelmine era, observed Kehr,
they had been staunchly monarchist and nationalist. Kehr
pointed out that from the beginning of the nineteenth century
these historians had been the intellectual leaders of the German
bourgeoisie and from decade to decade they had experienced
the same economic fate as the middle class as a whole. That is,
they had moved successively during that century from radical-
ism to moderate liberalism, then to an alliance with the
military monarchy and its policy of suppression of socialism
to a blatant imperialism; finally by 1933 the majority had
entered an alliance with fascism. This is an assessment which,
in view of the behaviour of the majority of historians in
Germany, is impossible to refute, though in many cases the

[1] Eckart Kehr, "Neuere Deutsche Geschichtsschreibung", in *Der
Primat der Innenpolitik,* ed. H. U. Wehler, p. 254.

alleged alliance with the Nazis was extremely uneasy and highly problematic.[2]

Kehr described the German history professor from the 1830's onward as having been a representative of middle class liberalism in its two forms. On the one hand it was believed that the individual in society was supposed to have the opportunity of free economic development to ensure his livelihood; on the other hand it was taught that the state should possess the possibility of unrestricted development to ensure its security. In short, freedom for the individual and power for the state were fundamental concepts of the academic historian until the 1870's. These two goals had been the object of their writings. But this so-called political school of historians collapsed because the German Reich was not founded by the bourgeoisie as they had originally expected in 1848, but by the military caste, the aristocracy and the Prussian state.

Nevertheless, with this development, a socio-economic order was achieved in which the liberal historians could at least concur. They were deprived of their political role, having been forced to look on as non-participants while their idea of the nation-state was incorporated in the Bismarckian constitution. Through this the German bourgeoisie, in contrast to the British and French, had no means of control over processes of political decision-making. They were, in the event, apparently content to see real power retained in the hands of the historic ruling classes. As a consequence, however, the historians gave up their liberalism which championed individual freedom together with

[2] Ibid., p. 255. See also Michael Stürmer, "Bismarcks Deutschland als Problem der Forschung" in *Das kaiserliche Deutschland—Politik und Gesellschaft 1870–1918*, ed. Michael Stürmer, p. 8. Stürmer elaborates on this theme indicating how the achievements of Bismarck culminating in 1871, "forced the liberals of all persuasions to accept *Realpolitik* as an historical norm as well as an historical yardstick. . . . History was understood as an educative as well as political force. But this development had two sides: historiography impressed its stamp on political culture but at the same time, both in its method as well as in its value-concepts, it fell also under the sway of the predominant liberal-conservative social influence."

advocating unlimited state power in order to champion the one component only — power.

The implications of these developments for the political education of the German people cannot be ignored. It is perhaps an overstatement of the case to suggest that this scholarly veneration of state power determined the course of German history, but how can one escape the reasonable conclusion that the long-term indoctrination of a particular political ideology — carried out with all the impressive argument of a well established scholarly tradition — did not have a formative influence on the political will of the German people?

In the Wilhelmine era the alliance between the occupants of the major chairs of history and members of the ruling classes, both on a personal and ideological plane, was most apparent. At the very least the dominant school of historians reinforced the political concepts and goals of the German governments. They popularised and justified the aims of German imperialism with obvious enthusiasm. But beyond this in the peculiar *Wechselwirkung* (reciprocal effect) relationship between historiography and politics, the professors not only prescribed the ideology in the framework of which political decisions were to be taken but even the political programme itself. History was for them literally political science. Historians had assumed the tasks of *politisches Vorausdenken* (i.e. "thinking out the lines of policy in advance") and were recognised in this role.[3]

In the sultry intellectual climate of Wilhelmine Germany the political commentaries of the academics, especially the historians, could not fail to have a formative influence on the assumptions and values of politicians and statesmen. Fritz Ringer has illustrated this supremely well in his recent work,

[3] c.f. Waldemar Besson, "Geschichte als politische Wissenschaft", in *Geschichte und Gegenwartsbewusstsein,* eds. W. Besson and F. Hiller von Gaertringen, pp. 71, 75–6. Besson observes, however, that although historians in Germany around the turn of the century thought of themselves in this role, they lost their essentially critical function and became merely handmaids of the predominant forces and tendencies in society. They continued to point the direction of policy but had become so Germano-centric that they lost all true perspective on political reality.

The Decline of the German Mandarins.[4] Particularly after 1890, "many German academics had come to assume the stance of Platonic philosopher-statesmen preparing to meet the onslaught of the mechanics".[5] The word "mechanics" in this context alludes to the working class and their political representatives, the German Social Democratic Party which was certainly regarded as a towering threat to the monarchical-conservative system which the academics championed. But beyond this the word also characterises the German view of the western democracies whose "mechanistic" view of society, and its extension around the globe, chiefly in the form of the British Empire was regarded as a threat to the "German idea" and its mission in the world. The plain fact is that both imperial German domestic and foreign policy is only intelligible against the *Weltanschauung* constructed by German philosophers and historians during the earlier nineteenth century which had been adapted and applied by their spiritual descendants at the end of the century.

As far as the historians were concerned — and here they are the critical group of academics whose doctrines impinge directly on politics — the great nineteenth century figure whose *Weltanschauung* was adapted and applied was Leopold von Ranke (1795–1886). The influence of his ideas concerning the nature of state power was immense. It is not without significance that a famous German scholar, Hermann Kantorowicz (1877–1940), while in exile in the United States during the 1930's, pointed out to his American students that there was an important distinction between thoughts and ideas. *Men possessed thoughts, but ideas possessed men.*[6] In the German

[4] Fritz Ringer, *The Decline of the German Mandarins.*

[5] Ibid., pp. 123–4.

[6] Max Lerner, *Ideas are Weapons—The History and Use of Ideas,* p. 3. In this connection Carl Becker's famous article "What is Historiography?" *AHR* XLIVC (1938) is very instructive. One of his main points is that it is essential for historiographers "to know what ideas, true or false, were at any time accepted and what pressure they exerted upon those who entertained them" (p. 26). So ideas, whether rational or irrational, which caused men to act have of necessity to be investigated since without them nothing approaching a full explanation can be achieved.

intellectual context which Ringer described, it is easy to grasp how readily an "idea", which had been recognised by scientific (wissenschaftlich) means as being valid, could take on the character of unassailable dogmatic truth for the educated German.[7] And because the historians were imprisoned by an idea which was believed to be of eternal validity, they in turn imposed their concepts upon virtually the entire nation. Essentially, the idea which took possession of Germans before 1914 (and, indeed, still later) was that concerning the nature of state power. And the chief sustainers and propagators of this idea at the turn of the century were the so-called Neo-Rankean historians.

A contemporary East German scholar, Hans Schleier, has recently pointed to the great influence exerted by the Neo-Rankean school prior to the Great War.[8] They had by the turn of the century completely superseded the previously dominant school, namely the Prussian, whose greatest champion had been the famous Heinrich von Treitschke. In displacing the Prussian school whose "nation-building work" had in a sense been accomplished, the Neo-Rankeans claimed the "monopoly of scholarship" (Monopol der Wissenschaftlichkeit) and secured general recognition of their position as the undisputed historical authority in Germany.[9] It is the "self-understanding" of the Neo-Rankean school and the political implications of its doctrines which are of interest here.

The Prussian school which the Neo-Rankeans displaced had regarded the final establishment of German unity in 1871 essentially as "their work". That is to say, the victory of Prussia over the remainder of "Germany" which had been preached by J. G. Droysen and his followers from the 1850's onwards was seen as having been effectively prepared by means of their influential teaching.[10] They had, in short, mobilised the political will of the nation to pave the way for Bismarck's final success.

[7] c.f. Georg G. Iggers, The German Conception of History, p. 12.

[8] Hans Schleier, "Die Ranke-Renaissance", in Die bürgerliche deutsche Geschichtsschreibung von der Reichseinigung von oben bis zur Befreiung Deutschlands vom Fachismus, ed. J. Streisand, p. 104.

[9] Ibid., p. 103.

[10] Besson, "Geschichte als politische Wissenschaft", p. 70.

After that achievement was realised the Prussian school then saw its national task in consolidating the idea of a Prussian-dominated Germany in the hearts and minds of all subjects of the new Reich. This, indeed, was the declared aim of Heinrich von Treitschke's famous history of Germany in the nineteenth century.[11]

However, these remarkably one-sided interpretations of German history were the cause of a certain amount of disquiet among the younger generation of historians emerging in the 1880's and 1890's who, of course, had in many instances been the pupils of the famous Prussians. These younger men led by Max Lenz (1850–1932) and Erich Marcks (1861–1938) began to feel that it was now time to give up writing history inspired by emotional desires to realise narrow political goals, and return to the objective universal approach established by Leopold von Ranke. As Lenz himself expressed it:

> As long as the nation was engaged in the struggle for its supreme values, objective history had to recede; when the victory had been achieved it returned of its own (*von selbst*). The passions have been satisfied and so once again we can exercise justice.[12]

Heinrich Ritter von Srbik in his assessment of this phenomenon commented:

> History gradually lost the great echo of the period of the German struggles. It sacrificed its more popular appeal (*Volksnähe*) and fervour (*Leuchtstärke*) but it became more scholarly as it liberated itself from the national historical legend.[13]

Srbik went on to note that at the turn of the century German historiography was striving to combine its duty to the nation with its duty to scholarship.[14] This admission by the notable Austrian historian that men of learning have indeed other

[11] See Treitschke's dedicatory remarks to his friend Max Duncker in the preface to the former's *History of Germany in the Nineteenth Century*, pp. xiii–xv.

[12] Schleier, "Die Ranke-Renaissance", p. 105. See also Hans-Heinz Krill, *Die Ranke-Renaissance*, p. 12.

[13] Heinrich Ritter von Srbik, *Geist und Geschichte*, 2nd ed., Vol. II, p. 2.

[14] Ibid., p. 3.

obligations than to the relentless pursuit of knowledge rather tends to confirm the judgment of Hermann Kantorowicz concerning the attitude of continental historians towards truth.

This alleged movement towards a more scholarly, objective and "universal" approach to history as opposed to the more narrow, purely nationalist approach was centred around a revival of Leopold von Ranke's historiographical principles. Max Lenz, for example, began to celebrate Ranke as the "greatest of all historians" and the "educator of the German nation to historical thinking".[15]

Basic to Ranke's conception of history was the idea of nation-states as historical individualities each one with its own personality — an organic unity which was striving to develop and, of course, preserve itself in competition with its neighbours. History was concerned with the development of these unique personalities and their interaction with each other. This is the "universal" component in Ranke's thinking which attracted Lenz and his colleagues. Of course, the interaction of states which Ranke had observed in this day had been confined to the old established European Powers. However, by 1900 these Powers had expanded dramatically throughout the globe to become empires or "world-states". It was the observation of this fact which encouraged Lenz to apply, rather optimistically, the Rankean doctrine of the eternal struggle for the balance of power to the modern system of world states. What could be more logical for a German historian since the German people had now entered the association of the Great Powers than to turn his attention to the activity of the concert of powers as Ranke had done earlier? For this reason Ranke's "universalist" view of history was re-invoked, and that meant in practice the study of hegemonial struggles of the imperialist Powers.

Ranke's conception of the behaviour of nation-states as being in constant rivalry with each other was expressed in 1833 in his famous essay *The Great Powers,* and subsequently (in 1836) reinforced in a paper entitled *The Political Dialogue.*[16] Max

[15] Ibid., pp. 6–7.

[16] c.f. Theodor von Laue, *Leopold Ranke—the Formative Years,* pp. 152–218.

Lenz regarded these texts as containing the "sum of modern history and therefore the basis of all policy".[17]

Clearly the "young Rankeans", as Karl Lamprecht ironically labelled them,[18] believed they had identified with Ranke's aid the operative forces of history which had an eternal validity like Kepler's laws.[19] Indeed, the young Rankeans regarded themselves as being in possession of the only valid method of historical enquiry and were extremely successful in expanding and consolidating their influence over German historiography. This, of course, was made possible by the fact that numerous other established historians already held Ranke in high esteem and this enabled the doctrinaire Neo-Rankeans (*die Methodiker*) among the conservative Ranke supporters to stir up and dominate a virtual Ranke renaissance which flourished right into the period of the First World War.[20]

It will, of course, be obvious that among so many historians there existed various categories of Ranke supporters, but in general two main groups can be identified: a conservative stream and a moderate liberal stream. The conservatives were led by Max Lenz, Erich Marcks and Felix Rachfal. These exerted great influence over many students who in turn became practising historians. The moderate liberals counted such notable professors as Hermann Oncken, Friedrich Meinecke and Hans Delbrück in their ranks but even these had essentially conservative beginnings.[21]

It is important to note that while the two streams held divergent views regarding the issues of domestic policy such as parliamentarianism and the labour movement, there was very little to distinguish them in their attitude towards foreign policy; both streams supported an energetic imperialist and "world policy".[22] This is no doubt due to the common acceptance of the Rankean doctrine concerning the character of nation-states.

Essentially, a state was the product of the unique historical experience of a *Volk*. Humanity as part of the divine plan (Ranke was, of course, a religious man trained in Lutheran

[17] Schleier, "Die Ranke-Renaissance", pp. 102–3.   [18] Ibid., p. 102.
[19] Ibid.   [20] Ibid., p. 120.   [21] Ibid.   [22] Ibid., p. 104.

theology) was divided up into various nations. Each nation possessed a unique spirit which had earlier been identified by Herder as the *Volksgeist*. This revealed itself in the various cultural characteristics peculiar to a people. So a people or *Volk* was a unique historical individuality which strove to preserve its identity in competition with neighbouring peoples. The degree of success which a people enjoyed in preserving its identity was dependent upon what Ranke termed its "moral energy". This can be understood as the manner in which a people asserted itself against the encroachment of its neighbours. Indeed, an essential property of a *Volk* was the principle of organic growth of the innate desire to expand at the expense of weaker neighbours, i.e. neighbours whose "moral energy" was inferior.

There are several points regarding Ranke's understanding of the character of nations which must be summarised here. First, states, i.e. the political expression of "peoples", are part of the divine plan for mankind. Second, states are *ipso facto* expansionist, since they must grow if they are not to be eclipsed by their stronger neighbours. Third, because of this, the most important factor in the life of a state is its foreign policy, hence the Rankean doctrine of the *Primat der Aussenpolitik*. Fourth, because a state is a unique organism which proceeds in the world according to its own laws of development, it is compelled to resort to war in order to survive. "War, indeed, was the father of all things", said Ranke quoting Heraclitus. It was in fact the motor of history.[23] Out of it emerged progress because it was the supreme test of the moral energies of the competing nations; those who generated the stronger energy prevailed, the others declined. The course of modern history had shown plainly that this was the case. However, nations resisted extinction with great tenacity. Whenever a smaller power was threatened by a greater, it always sought an alliance with the next available state or states so that together they could combine their energies to resist the threat of extinction.

[23] Leopold von Ranke, *Die Grossen Mächte—Politisches Gespräch*, p. 37.

Ranke had observed that since the time of Louis XIV this process had been in evidence. Whenever a single power emerged so strong as to threaten to establish an hegemony over the others, these would coalesce and, if necessary, wage war against the so-called hegemonial power. The example of this which Ranke personally observed in his youth was the series of anti-Napoleonic coalitions in the period 1809 to 1815. So, for him the apparently confused spectacle of changing alliances and their resultant wars among the European peoples was really the working out of a unique logic.[24] The Concert of Europe was a system wrought by a series of historical emergencies; there was nothing fortuitous about it. It was all a function of the need of the various states at once to expand if possible and to preserve their identity. And further, underlying it all despite the existence of war, was an essential harmony; the balance of power was maintained together with the identity of each *Volk*. And since the various peoples were expressions of the divine will, they all had a right to survive. Ranke was opposed to the idea of one superpower crushing all the rest.

Finally, Ranke (in contrast to Hegel) would not admit that war was part of the divine plan. It was simply stark necessity which compelled states to go to war. So Ranke, always refusing to abandon his religious belief in a moral law, never resolved the dilemma which emerged from his scheme of world history. The divine plan envisaged the competition of the various nation-states which of necessity often resulted in war, but God did not employ evil (as Hegel would have it) in the working out of His purpose for mankind.[25] It was this unfortunate equivocation by Ranke on the subject of war, national expansion and morality which led his admirers at the turn of the century to entertain reckless schemes for German aggrandisement.

The historical "method" based on the above Rankean scheme was developed by Max Lenz and his colleagues into a veritable ideology of *Weltpolitik* in the conviction that they were being wholly impartial and objective. However, so personally con-

[24] Ibid., pp. 41–42.
[25] von Laue, *Leopold Ranke,* p. 87.

cerned were they with the fate of the fatherland that their historical writing — especially on the nineteenth century and contemporary history — reveals a strongly teleological component.[26] Their undeclared aim was to promote the power and prestige of the German Reich in the world.

Hans-Heinz Krill in his work on the Ranke renaissance lays bare the steps in the thought of the chief inspirers of the movement. Reflecting on the history of European expansion in the nineteenth century, the Neo-Rankeans during the 1890's concluded that this phenomenon was due to the effects of the "nationality idea" which had its roots in the French Revolution. The decisive characteristic of this was the drive to expansion which every nation experienced having become conscious of its identity. In short, the ideals of 1789 had for the first time released forces which had led the European nations to unprecedented heights of power. Following their inherent drive for expansion they had succeeded with the accumulation of power (generated obviously through their energetic competition) in carrying European culture to the four corners of the globe. Max Lenz saw in this a confirmation of Ranke's observation that the spirit of the Orient had paled before the culture of the European nations.[27] The belief in the innate superiority of European over non-European culture is central to Lenz's thought. Only by accepting and imitating the fruits of European culture could other races hope "to rescue themselves".[28] In other words, the non-European peoples would have to develop a national consciousness in the way the Europeans had done since 1789 and in doing so would begin to generate the "moral energy" necessary to liberate and assert themselves.

As far as the Powers themselves were concerned, it was observed in 1900 that each of them was striving to expand until some external force caused this "organic" process of expansion

[26] Schleier, "Die Ranke-Renaissance", p. 106. c.f. M. C. Brands, *Historisme als Ideologie: Het 'Anti-Normative' en 'onpolitieke' Element in de Duitse Geschiedwetenschap*, p. 258.

[27] Krill, *Die Ranke-Renaissance*, p. 174.

[28] Ibid.

to halt. It was because of the absence of a counter-pressure that such states as the U.S.A., China, Britain and Russia had been able to expand to the extent which they did.

It was then reasoned that Germany, too, must be subject to the same law. Did not Germany in her medieval past expand ruthlessly at the cost of weaker neighbours? So the reason why Germany was apparently non-expansionist at the turn of the century must have been because her natural drive for expansion was being restricted by the strength of the surrounding powers.

There is clearly no place for concepts of traditional morality or international law in the Neo-Rankean scheme. These are ignored in order to sanction an active policy of expansion — a policy which must be pursued because the Powers are locked in an imperialist struggle for existence.[29] But it must be observed that power could not be considered as intrinsically evil by the Neo-Rankeans as, for example, Lord Acton regarded it. The dazzling spectacle of Imperial Germany's power was for them the logical extension of the moral, spiritual and cultural elements of Prusso-German history. These things were the prerequisites of state power. Essentially, the state was the natural synthesis of the moral, spiritual and cultural heritage of the *Volk*. As such, states, as Ranke maintained, were "ideas of God", unique individualities with a spiritual role to fulfil. In this way, the essence of state power, far from being corrupting, as Acton said, was idealised. For the Neo-Rankeans the state was the synthesis between *Macht* and *Geist* — power and spirit. Therefore, to apply the moral concepts of natural law to the behaviour of states was totally irrelevant — they were subject to their own (divine) unique laws of motion only.

In expanding these ideas in 1900 in a paper entitled *Ein Blick in das zwanzigste Jahrhundert* (A look into the 20th century), Max Lenz declared quite openly that "we will grasp out around us once again as soon as there is a power for us to divide such as in the case of Poland one hundred years ago".[30] Further, Lenz made the point that historians would no longer seek to

29 Ibid., p. 175.
30 Ibid.

identify aggressors, i.e. make moral condemnations of the state which allegedly broke the international peace. This is because all the Powers by their very nature were aggressors. Lenz illustrated this by pointing to Britain's war against the Boers. And in their relationships to each other the Great Powers were locked in a "constant struggle for existence and power".[31] There were thus no international friends — only rivals and antagonists. This was the unalterable norm of political life.

Dr. Krill in his searching analysis of Lenz's thought queries whether, having made these depressing observations, he was in any way disturbed by the existence of the few superpowers. Lenz asserted that as the examples of the Crimean and Boer wars had shown, "the political energy of those world empires (*Weltreiche*) was not exactly in relationship to their extent".[32] By this Lenz simply meant that geographical size did not automatically imply real power. This comforting observation was supported by applying Seeley's concept that the stronger the pressure on a country from outside, the stronger tended to be the counter-pressure built up from within that country to resist. Therefore, it was the smaller powers which tended to profit from this situation. Clearly, Lenz had in mind the central position occupied by Germany in Europe. Here his historical model was Prussia which had been a "glorious example" of the creative force of pressure from without. Surrounded as she was by antagonists, Prussia had been compelled to generate and concentrate her energy in order to survive. Her expansionist policy had been the 'organic' response to those external pressures.

Equipped with these convictions Lenz sought to explain the contemporary phenomenon of imperialism. He saw Europe as a tiny field occupied by a group of energetic rivals which had in their competition for power developed the highest degree of political energy the world had ever seen. This was clear since they had succeeded in subjugating virtually the entire earth. But this process of European expansion into the power vacuums of the world was the result of the mutual pressure of the European

[31] Ibid.
[32] Ibid.

powers on each other. They were merely following their persistent drive for expansion which the energies they had accumulated in constant friction with each other had generated.

These observations had convinced Lenz of the absolute validity of Ranke's "laws" for the entire global scene, i.e. also for the extra-European states of the future. Thus armed with the immutable laws of history, Lenz concentrated his attention on the international political ferment of his day. He was further convinced that the ideas of the past would continue to maintain their validity for the future if only the European nations did not disintegrate from within. There was a danger of this from revolutionary ideologies which would tend to erode the moral energies of the nations. This was a very conservative and Eurocentric view of world history, but at the time the Neo-Rankeans believed they saw their concepts confirmed everywhere.

The world by 1900 had been effectively colonised by the European powers. This colonisation process was due to the overflowing moral energy of the various European nationalities. These had imposed their political and cultural will upon numerous lesser peoples not only overseas but even within Europe itself. Now this imposition of hegemony on weaker nations was seen logically, if the Rankean scheme was valid, to cause the moral energy of the suppressed peoples to surge up — the natural organic response to outside pressure.

It should be recalled here that when Herder had laid the foundations of modern German historiography his chief emphasis was on the "nationality principle" or the development of the unique *Volksgeist*. This concern with the emergence of the nationalities was the central element in the growth of German historicism (or historism), as Friedrich Meinecke has pointed out in his work *Die Entstehung des Historismus*.[33] Therefore, the political thought of the Neo-Rankeans was determined by the nationality principle. Everywhere in the world around 1900 they saw suppressed nationalities awakening. In Europe this took the form of the growing national particularism of such peoples as the Poles, the Flemings and the Castillians

[33] (Munich, 1965), passim.

who were resentful of the domination of a more powerful nationality.[34] Outside Europe the situation was even more dramatic; in the British Empire many examples of nationalities awakening could be seen rising up against the predominance of the English cultural heritage. Prophetically Lenz saw the structure of the British Empire being most threatened by the upsurge of the nationality idea. The anglicisation policies being pursued in vain by Britain in Malta and South Africa illustrated the essential validity of the nationality idea. However, Lenz was convinced that for the suppressed nationalities to be successful in their struggle for independence they would have to adopt the external forms of the triumphant European civilization. The Japanese had entered the ranks of the Powers by doing just that; those, such as the Indians and Chinese, who were as yet incapable of adopting European civilization, would have to succumb to it.[35]

The attraction of these arguments as they were put forward in 1900 can well be appreciated. The world indeed presented such an aspect when observed from Berlin. Everywhere there was a perceptible extension of European civilization. But this had a reciprocal effect on the suppressed nationalities; under these conditions they grew more aware of their own historic identity and strove for independence. This process was inexorable; the pressure of the Great Powers on weaker nationalities provoked the growth of those "moral energies" (namely the will, ambition and determination to become independent of the oppressors) which heralded the emergence of new nations.

The rise of new nation-states through struggle against their erstwhile colonial masters was, according to Lenz in 1900, to become the chief characteristic of the twentieth century. The reciprocal action of the nationality idea with the spread of European civilization was about complete. That is to say, the impact of the imperialist Powers on the colonised peoples had reached that stage where a large number of young or rejuven-

[34] Krill, *Die Ranke-Renaissance*, p. 178. It is curious to note the omission of the case of Germany's ally, the Austro-Hungarian empire.
[35] Ibid., p. 179.

ated nations were stirring themselves to challenge their oppressors.

The most obvious examples of this development were to be found in the British Empire, and a war among the Great Powers themselves would provide the supreme test of the power and cohesiveness of the British as well as the Russian and other empires. This was because the colonial peoples would in such an event seize the opportunity to rise up in arms against their imperial masters because they had sensed their impending decline.[36]

Doubtless beneath this reasoning was the wish to see British power in particular dissolved or reduced. However, while Lenz recognised the remote possibility of a weakening of the European Powers resulting from imperialist conflict, he was at the same time convinced of their political realism. They would see the long-term dangers implicit in an armed aggression and would do all in their power to avoid it. That is to say, if the relations between the European Powers became strained as a result of friction over their African or Asian interests and possessions, they would shy back from war with each other, since this would not only shatter the basis of European civilization but also lose them their colonies and therewith the predominance of European Powers in the world.[37]

In this scheme of things the stability of the world was but delicately preserved. A breakdown in European diplomacy could lead to a world conflagration and an upheaval of the old order of incalculable dimensions. A war of this scale which would throw all into the balance was thus always a real possibility. It would be the natural result of the expansionist drive of the Powers in constant rivalry interacting with the independence movements being generated in the colonies. How then, in the Neo-Rankean scheme, was peace maintained? In answering this Lenz and his supporters were acting as the true "heralds of policy". Peace was secured through a mighty buildup of armaments which would act as a deterrent and thus be

[36] Ibid., p. 181.
[37] Ibid., p. 184.

the best guarantee of peace. Further, since the Neo-Rankeans never repudiated Bismarckian *Realpolitik,* it was observed with satisfaction that there were still sufficient weak states available in which the Powers could expend their energies without clashing with each other. And even if clashes of the Powers occurred, this still did not mean the ignition of war, "otherwise Europe would be permanently in flames".[38] Tensions could be relieved through conferences of the Powers, and disputes could be arbitrated. Also it occurred often enough that two disputing powers could settle their differences at the expense of a third weaker state. These, then, were the means by which world peace was maintained. The task to be pursued by Germany in these circumstances was simply the consolidation and, where possible, the extension of her power. In short, she must be strong enough to "command the peace" (*den Frieden zu befehlen*).[39] This was necessary because the late-comer, Germany, needed peaceful conditions in order to be able to gain anything at all in the imperialistic rivalry among what were essentially aggressive super-states. So a "healthy" power-policy by Germany in those "cold war" conditions at the turn of the century had the virtue of providing some prospects of territorial gain. Indeed, no power came too late on the imperialist scene provided it was strong enough to demand something. Armaments, therefore, served the dual function of ensuring peace and of enabling Germany's influence to be extended throughout the world.

The hidden argument for the preservation of peace was primarily the inherent danger of a world war breaking out as a result of friction among the Powers in the colonial sphere. It was nothing short of risking the self-destruction of both European power and civilization. This, indeed, was the terrible fate envisaged by German political thinking if the system of the imperialist balance of power should break down — in short the alternative to pursuing an imperialist policy based on a massive armaments programme. Such was the calculation which not only Neo-Rankeans made with their persuasive reasoning; it was also clearly the policy of the government.

[38] Ibid.   [39] Ibid., p. 185.

The basic idea of Tirpitz's policy of naval armament, for example, was to establish a balance of power at sea to offset the apparent British hegemony. The questions which are raised here are central for understanding the function of political historiography. Were the Neo-Rankeans merely describing and analysing what the great naval leader had designed on his own initiative? Was Tirpitz, in other words, a figure with the same olympian traits as Bismarck — a man of destiny pioneering the way into the future for the Reich? Or was it that Tirpitz merely translated into action the ideas he acquired from his well-known interest in modern German history and through his friendship with famous German historians? Who, indeed, was the real initiator of German policy? At the very least we have here to deal with an obvious reciprocal relationship between historiography and politics.

The historian for his part prepared a general political conception based on his understanding of the historical function of states in relation to each other and this conception was applied to the needs of the nation by the practising statesmen. In this instance the application was made with such inexorable logic that one cannot escape the observation that German historiography contained a political programme. There was, in short, full agreement between the chief formulators of political will in the community and actual government policy.

This is illustrated by a comparison of statements justifying naval armament by the historians on one hand and the political leaders on the other. It will be clear that the historians regarded German imperialist policy in general, as well as the Tirpitz fleet in particular, as purely defensive. They wanted nothing more than to see Germany grow into her "necessary" position of world power without wishing to exercise a hegemony. Logically, of course, the Neo-Rankeans had to oppose the idea of Germany becoming a hegemonial power like Napoleonic France because this would only provoke a vast coalition of enemies against Germany. So Germany merely wished to become an "equal among the firsts"[40] — in order to preserve the balance of power.

[40] Ibid., p. 196.

This rationale was advanced to justify the building of the battle fleet. Such a step was necessary to ensure Germany's freedom of movement and ready access to world markets. In this way the central nerve of Britain's power would be threatened — necessary because Britain was striving with all her might to establish a hegemony around the world. By suppressing the freedom of millions of subject peoples this policy was endangering world peace.

Arguments of the same content were put forward by the Kaiser in 1898 when he proclaimed German protection over three hundred million Moslems; the fleet was necessary to lend force to this claim and give Germany that prestige in the world which only a mighty and manoeuvrable naval arm could achieve. In addition to the Kaiser's motives, those of Tirpitz himself reveal a definite Neo-Rankean content. The admiral was of the opinion that the immense growth of Britain and Russia was destroying the "balance in the world" and this had to be restored by Germany by means of the fleet. In short, Germany had an obligation to arm in this way to maintain world peace.[41] As Krill observes, the coincidence between the political content of German historiography at that time with official policy is demonstrated here to the point of absurdity.[42] As recent commentators have shown, the preoccupation of most German historians before 1914 with the question of Germany's position of power in the world was extreme. They were convinced of the historical necessity of a German world

[41] Ibid., p. 202. A confirmation of Tirpitz's distinctly Neo-Rankean conception of world politics can be seen in his *Immediatvortrag* of 28 September 1899 to the Kaiser in which he outlines his reasons for the Second Navy Law. The theme is that Germany was locked in competition with the other Great Powers, Russia, Britain, and the United States of America. All were expanding. It was therefore vital for Germany to arm with a battle fleet if she was not to go under. On the other hand if Germany could build up sufficient naval strength to challenge Britain's power at sea, the latter would lose any inclination to attack Germany, and so the Reich would have a free hand to conduct a more expansionist policy overseas. I am indebted to Dr. Paul Kennedy of the University of East Anglia for drawing my attention to this document.

[42] Krill, *Die Ranke-Renaissance,* p. 202.

mission and never tired of proclaiming it.[43] The extent to which the German public was affected by the voluminous writing and teaching about *Weltpolitik* was recognised by none other than Sir Eyre Crowe at the time when he said that no responsible German statesman with the exception of a second Bismarck could have executed a policy which would have required the cessation of German naval building.[44] This had become an essential component in the Neo-Rankean understanding of Germany's foreign policy role and had been hammered home in the minds of the public with enormous effect. But it was not that the policy-makers were too afraid to go against public opinion; they, too, were dominated by the Neo-Rankean world of ideas as recent research has shown. Alternatives to that "system" could simply not be envisaged as the next chapter seeks to illustrate.

[43] Willy Schenk, *Die deutsch-englische Rivalität vor dem ersten Weltkrieg in der Sicht deutscher Historiker*, p. 157.
[44] Ibid., p. 9 (n.).

CHAPTER II

Kurt Riezler and *Weltpolitik*

> Bethmann and Riezler genuinely believed that fate or
> a concatenation of deep forces in world history was
> thrusting world dominance upon Germany.
>
> FRITZ STERN[1]

Riezler published two widely read books before 1914. The first
was entitled *Die Erforderlichkeit des Unmöglichen, Prolego-
mena zu einer Theorie der Politik und zu anderen Theorien*
(1913). The second was published a year later under the
pseudonym of J. J. Ruedorffer with the title, *Grundzüge der
Weltpolitik in der Gegenwart*.[2] It is profitable to assess the
historical–philosophical content of these works and to see with
the help of the diary if these conceptions were operating on the
Chancellor at the time of the outbreak of war.

The above-mentioned books of Riezler presented his view
of the world as he saw it in 1912–1914. What strikes one
immediately as Rankean is the concept of the *Volk* and *Staat*.
In contrast to the more rational, mechanistic Western view of
the nation, the nation or *Volk* in Riezler's work remains
nebulous; he employs "organic" imagery such as "tree" and
"wave" etc.[3] The same kind of imagery was presented in
Herder's writings and it re-emerges strongly in the work of
Ranke where the concept of organic growth as in vegetation is
applied to the community of the *Volk*.[4] Further, as was the

---

[1] Stern, "Bethmann Hollweg and the War", p. 272.
[2] c.f. Geiss, *Die Erforderlichkeit*, p. 55.
[3] Ibid.
[4] c.f. Srbik, *Geist und Geschichte*, I, pp. 138–143, 251–259.

case with Hegel, Riezler identifies the state as being based on
a coincidence of geography, race and culture. All ethnic groups
living in a circumscribed region evolved with their own unique
culture and strove to develop a distinct political life as a
"State".[5]

Riezler's indebtedness to Herder, Hegel and Ranke, the
founders of the "German conception of history",[6] becomes
more and more evident. There is an emphasis on racial affinity
as being a pre-requisite for the foundation of a nation and that
people of the same race strive to become a "nation" and only
absorb foreign minorities in so far as these do not pose a threat
to the racial purity of the nation.[7]

However, more important for the present theme is Riezler's
understanding of international relations. And here the Neo-
Rankean (more than social Darwinist) component is undeniable. Eternal peace is not regarded as either attainable or
even desirable.[8] It is in the nature of each state to expand until
it meets with immovable resistance; stronger states naturally
have prior rights over weaker states. This, too, is based on the
concept of the *Volk* which, like a wave in the sea, strives to
become even higher! There is a restless inborn striving in
nations which drives them on to a limitless expansion.[9] As
Riezler stated:

> . . . each people wants to grow, expand, dominate and subjugate
> others without end, wants to make itself more and more cohesive
> and to incorporate more and more within itself to become a higher
> totality until the world has become an organic unity under its
> domination.[10]

[5] c.f. Friedrich Meinecke, *Die Idee der Staatsräson in der neueren
Geschichte,* pp. 403–433, and also his *Weltbürgertum und Nationalstaat,*
pp. 237–238.

[6] c.f. Iggers, *Die deutsche Geschichtswissenschaft,* passim.

[7] Geiss, *Die Erforderlichkeit,* p. 56.

[8] Ranke, *Die Grossen Mächte,* p. 37 and pp. 41–43. c.f. Meinecke,
Staatsräson, p. 411. Note Meinecke's discussion of the nature of the
state, pp. 237–239. The neo-Rankean contemporaries of Kurt Riezler
propagated this view of the state at the turn of the century. See Krill,
Die Ranke-Renaissance, p. 175.

[9] Geiss, *Die Erforderlichkeit,* p. 56.   [10] Ibid.

So, according to Riezler, there must be constant struggle for the attainment of world domination which is allegedly the goal of all peoples. This is illustrated by pointing to the history of the subjugation of the Poles in the eastern marches of Prussia.[11] And in a world so ordered there is no room for such concepts as the protection of the weak. There is no such thing as peaceful coexistence of equally privileged states; there are no international friends, only rivals; hostility is the supreme principle.[12] Riezler expressed it thus:

> Nations may proceed in friendship alongside each other for centuries if their paths do not cross; however, at some stage . . . they must, if they continue to strive ahead, finally confront each other in hostility. This is because they are all striving towards the same goal; therefore the attainment of that goal by one, means the decline (Untergang) of the other. So any friendship between nations is only a postponement of hostility . . .[13]

Riezler elaborated this by saying that the available space for expansion was limited and therefore if the nations did not want to mark time, there was a limit to the number of times that the final reckoning could be postponed.[14]

What we have here is really the ideological justification for German aspirations of world power; there is in all states the drive for limitless expansion because they all desire world domination. In this scheme of things war is not only legitimate but natural.[15] So, like the Hegelian, Rankean and Neo-Rankean philosophy of history, Riezler's philosophy was an affirmation of war. And of the consequences of this Riezler was well aware; he foresaw the coming situation very clearly. International law and treaties were simply the formal documentation of the postponement of hostility and such things could be discarded for example, like "scraps of paper" when it served the interests of the state to do so.

This concept of treaties being only a postponement of hostility was developed further by Riezler in his Ruedorffer book. Here above all the Neo-Rankean strain in his thought

---

[11] Ibid., p. 57.   [12] Ibid., c.f. Krill, *Die Ranke-Renaissance*, p. 175.
[13] Ibid.   [14] Ibid.   [15] Ibid., p. 58.

dominates. As well as treaties and international law, the so-called "constellation" within the world imperialistic system, i.e. the constant re-shaping of alliances to maintain the balance of power, served to put off the day of final reckoning. Here Riezler offers practical guidelines for German world policy. It was necessary, he maintained, for Germany to be strongly armed because armaments (as deterrents) were the modern means of postponement.[16] *Die Rüstungen sind die moderne Form des Aufschubs,*[17] (and) *unser Zeitalter ist das der grössten Kriegsrüstungen und des längsten Friedens.*[18] The parallel with the teachings of Max Lenz is too close to be merely coincidental. What Riezler says about the armaments race is already adumbrated by Lenz. It was not true that the Powers armed themselves to no purpose or that their armament was not in some way employed. Admittedly, wars are not meant to be fought but they are *calculated* for.

> The cannon do not fire but they have a voice in the negotiations. The procedure of estimating one's own military power and that of the opponent decides, together with other associated factors in the context of the overall diplomatic situation, the degree of concessions which one has to make or one is able to demand from one's opponents. This estimation is, however, the calculation of war.[19]

Clearly, the purpose of armaments is to enforce concessions without actually employing them. A superiority in capability is to be achieved not so much to fight victorious wars as to be able to confront the possibility of them and to cause the opposition to do the same.[20] It was, according to Riezler, the paradox of the times that the armaments race had replaced warfare. The reasoning behind this is given thus by Riezler:

> The overall calculation for war is composed of two separate calculations. One concerns the relation of the advantages of a victory to the cost of a victory on the one hand and to the cost of a defeat on the other. The second calculation concerns the probability relationship of victory to defeat. Armaments are the attempt to make this second calculation as favourable as possible. However, here a peculiar element enters in—the real dilemma

[16] Ibid., p. 59.   [17] Ruedorffer (Riezler), *Die Grundzüge,* p. 218.
[18] Ibid., p. 219.   [19] Ibid.   [20] Ibid.

of the armaments race—namely, that this attempt to make the second factor advantageous affects the first calculation in a way conducive to peace. Again there are two elements in the first calculation, namely the advantages of a victory and its *costs* in blood and treasure. The first of these two elements is constant. The second, however, which favours peace, is increased in importance through the general armaments race, because, with the growth of armaments grows the destructive capacity of wars, also for the victor. The more the nations arm the more the disproportion between the advantages of war and its disadvantages is altered in favour of the latter, and because of that, in favour of peace. A calculation for war can only then point to the usefulness of war if the disproportion in the first calculation in balanced out by a corresponding increase in the chances of victory over the risk of defeat in the second calculation. Or, the more the nations arm, the greater must be the superiority of one over the other if the calculation is to fall out in favour of a war.[21]

So argued Riezler, the likelihood of war between Powers was virtually non-existent because there was no possibility of real advantage being won; but there still existed the remote chance of war which could result from a diplomatic crisis where a power had manoeuvred itself into a situation where war was the only way out. This could come from "over-bluffing" in diplomacy. Bluffing, according to Riezler, was a key device in modern international relations. This resulted from the fact that if, in the relations between two disputing Powers, neither wanted to resort to war, it was not necessarily the more powerful which always won the contest of wills, but rather the one which could sustain the impression longer of being determined to resort to war! That is to say, the one which had the more patience, composure, persistence and cunning, even if objectively weaker, could always by bluffing cause the opposition to make concessions. However, in the constellation of alliances as they were in 1914, Riezler recognised the dangers implicit in this kind of brinkmanship.[22] A Power which had over-bluffed (*festgeblufft*) could find itself in a situation where it could not back out even if that Power recognised that it would be in its best interests to do so.

[21] Ibid., p. 220.   [22] Ibid., p. 222.

Considerations of personal interest, the ambition of government
leaders, or the storm of indignation to be expected from the
nationalists can bring about a war which objective interests alone
would never have justified. For this reason the danger of war in
our day lies in the domestic politics of those countries in which a
weak government is confronted by a strong nationalistic movement.[23]

If one applies the idea contained in this last paragraph to
the contemporary situation within the *Reich* and the Austro-
Hungarian empire, Riezler's statement takes on a prophetic
quality. Its significance as prophecy or as prescription will be
investigated below. The present point is, however, despite the
obvious dangers recognised by Riezler to be implicit in the
"constellation" and in this style of diplomacy, he persisted in
supporting the continuation of this system and style of international relations for Germany. This is because of the belief
that cosmopolitanism and internationalism were both utopian
and decadent; real cultural progress resulted only from the
relentless competition among states, i.e. in the clash of nationalities. Each one by its very nature strove to assert itself and
expand in the world at the expense of the others. The German
Reich was, as Riezler observed in 1914, expanding in population at the rate of over 800,000 annually,[24] and its economic
growth was correspondingly great. And Riezler proclaimed
that the economic growth must be followed by political growth.
"The enormous productive achievement of the upward-striving
nations compels the young Reich to pursue *Weltpolitik*."[25] The
fact that the energy of the German people which brought about
national unity in 1871 was still available and not being employed made it necessary for the German nation to find outlets
for its energy. Max Weber had made this point as early as 1895
in his famous Freiburg inaugural address, namely that the
achievements of 1871 were only a stage in a general expansionist
development. Thus Riezler in 1914:

[23] Ibid.
[24] Geiss, *Die Erforderlichkeit*, p. 61.
[25] Ruedorffer (Riezler), *Die Grundzüge*, p. 102.

The unification of Germany was on the one hand the conclusion of a national development, the fulfilment of the nation's desires. It was on the other hand the beginning of a new development, the germ of new, far-reaching desires. Just as in the strivings of an individual so there are no limits and no end to the desires of nations. With the emergence of world political interests, German nationalism has orientated itself to world policy. The demands of the German people for power and prestige not only in Europe but around the earth have risen rapidly.[26]

Riezler had argued that the German people had no alternative but to pursue a world policy because it was being hemmed in within Europe:

Weltpolitik must be pursued. The economic expansion and the lively will of the people are pressing outwards. German policy must escape from the vicious circle. It cannot opt for a purely continental policy. The task which this situation provides is the real foreign policy problem of the German Reich. Everything that happens can be regarded as an attempt to solve this problem. It is clear that the freedom of movement of the German Reich will be all the greater the more independent its continental position becomes from the constellation of powers. This situation demands first and foremost that the German Reich liberate itself from the *cauchemar des coalitions* which oppressed Bismarck. For this reason the first requirement of German *Weltpolitik* is that Germany become so strong on the Continent that it would still have the chance of victory over every possible constellation. Only then would it be able to withstand the repercussions of its world-political enterprises on the continental constellation. Indeed, there would be no repercussions if it were seen that Germany on the Continent is not vulnerable to attack with the prospect of success even by a coalition of its world political opponents. The decision on *Weltpolitik* will fall on the Continent.[27]

The parallel between these reflections and actual German policy is too clear to be overlooked. Reduced to a bald statement it appears as follows: German *Weltpolitik* has a priority to fulfil itself in the world because Germans are the most energetic people. However, the basis on the Continent is too narrow — Germany is cramped within unfavourable borders.

[26] Geiss, *Die Erforderlichkeit,* p. 61.
[27] Ibid., p. 62.

Therefore the Reich must expand this basis in order to be able to establish an adequate base for its dynamic world policy. The fundamental prerequisite was that the Reich liberate itself from the *cauchemar des coalitions*. And that at the beginning of 1914 meant the dissolution of the *Entente*.

Riezler did not spell out whether he wished this to take place by force, but given his *Weltanschauung* about the nature of power to expand to world domination, it can be assumed that Riezler was aware that this goal could only be achieved by going to war.[28] Further, the aim to make Germany strong enough to be able to confront a coalition of her world-political opponents could only have been achieved by combining the equivalent power of France, Russia, Britain and possibly the U.S.A. as well as Japan within Germany! To do this Germany would have to become a super-power, and this would have meant the elimination, neutralisation or conquest of one or the other world-political opponents, which, as history demonstrated, could not be accomplished without a war.[29]

Given the above ideas it would now be quite unhistorical to consider German policy in the July crisis of 1914 (and the official German plans to expand after a victorious war) in isolation from them, particularly in view of the fact that Kurt Riezler was a central participant in the formulation of German policy.[30] His two pre-war books provided the outline of Germany's actual aims, namely the achievement of a position of at least an equi-privileged world power for the German Reich.[31] It remains to be seen whether Riezler's historically derived philosophy of international relations was actually operating as the ideological basis of German diplomacy during the July–August crisis in 1914.

Professor Andreas Hillgruber is of the opinion that this was indeed so. He maintains that Riezler's views were basic to his understanding of the inevitability of wars and that the same ideas were basic to Bethmann Hollweg's understanding of international politics. To this inevitability the statesman had to bow when all other means of furthering policy were exhausted

[28] Ibid., p. 63.   [29] Ibid., p. 64.   [30] Ibid.   [31] Ibid.

in his efforts to achieve the goal towards which he had of necessity to strive.[32]

The constellation of Powers in August 1914 made the war inevitable, but, according to Hillgruber, Bethmann and Riezler did not accept this fatalistically. They determined to try and influence the unfavourable trend of events against Germany by making a rational analysis of the situation in order to master it. Riezler had observed from the two Balkan wars 1912 and 1913 that the Powers had "postponed" an armed confrontation. The reason in his view was that military defeat for a European power meant political ruin. Again, for this reason the Powers were compelled to maintain a high degree of armament, and this was the modern form of postponement. The result was a "balance of armament" and so peace prevailed. Concessions could only be wrung from opponents by means of the diplomatic bluff. And the diplomacy of an upward-striving power would employ this device with greater determination than that of a stagnating power whose diplomacy would be characterised by vacillation and nervousness. To be allied to such a Power constituted the real danger for the leadership of a Great Power.[33] It was in any case the duty of the statesman, according to Riezler, to continue to make precise observations of the tendencies in the constellation, and on these observations base his foreign policy. The application of these theories to the July crisis presented the following picture:

It has been observed by the German leadership that Russian power had been developing apace and that a confrontation between Slavdom and Germandom was, sooner or later, unavoidable. Bethmann Hollweg was firmly convinced of this.[34] Nevertheless, there was still a chance of warding off this danger if the Central Powers held firm. Decisive action by the Central Powers in a relatively favourable crisis situation would stop the "moral" decline and the constant diminution in the prestige of the Danube monarchy.[35] Such a success had indeed been registered by Russia's backing down in the Bosnian crisis of

[32] Hillgruber, "Riezlers Theorie", p. 337.
[33] Ibid., p. 340. [34] Ibid., p. 341. [35] Ibid.

1908–09 under pressure of the Central Powers. Unfortunately, however, developments since then had taken the reverse course. In the two Balkan wars of 1912 and 1913 the situation had clearly favoured Russia. This was because Russia's interests had been represented by the action of her smaller allies while she herself remained aloof from actual hostilities in order to be unencumbered at the peace negotiations. However, now, after 1913 if the Russian preponderance in the Balkans was to be removed, the alliance constellation of the lesser Powers there would have to be altered, and both Germans and Austrians were making efforts in that direction. Whether this aim could be achieved by diplomatic means alone was doubtful since Austria-Hungary, herself a stagnating power in Riezler's definition, had to demonstrate by means of force of arms that she still was a real Great Power. Therefore, a contest of arms in the Balkans at the next available opportunity seemed absolutely necessary despite the risk involved.[36]

The risk thereby increased was tolerable according to Riezler's theory because the Russian–Austro-Hungarian rivalry in the Balkans did not touch the interests of the other Great Powers to the same extent. Hence there was a chance after the achievement of a limited goal via the mediation of the other Powers, chiefly Britain and Germany, of reaching a new arrangement on the Balkans, this time different from 1912–13, in favour of the Danube Monarchy at the expense of Russia. The mediation of the less concerned Powers, however, should not begin too soon; rather, according to the bluff concept, one should calculate exactly to which degree of intensity the crisis might be driven. The view that a large war could be avoided was, according to Riezler, based on the conviction that no Great Power would take that decision because the adjustment in power relationships would be small and did not touch the vital interests of another Great Power. The improvement in Anglo-German relations signified in 1913–14 had to enhance the chances of the success of this calculation while at the same time considerably weakening Britain's link with the Franco-Russian alliance which was evident from mid-June, 1914.[37]

[36] Ibid., p. 342.   [37] Ibid.

It is Hillgruber's interpretation that Bethmann's policy towards Britain did not aim at maintaining Britain neutral so as to allow Germany a free hand to deal with Russia and France. Rather, Bethmann's aim was to keep Britain as a partner for negotiations in international crises, chiefly in mediation attempts which would support Austro-Hungarian action against Serbia and thus function in favour of the Central Powers. And overall, this would have resulted in a loosening of the ties between Britain and Russia. All these reflections led to Bethmann's calculation that if there was to be diplomatic test of strength with the Dual Alliance, the cause would have to be located in the Balkans, i.e. one in which Austria was involved with Germany behind her.[38]

Such was the calculated risk which Bethmann envisaged, but it was heightened not only as Riezler said by the indignation of the nationalists and expansionists within Germany who could force the Government to go further than the intended goal, but also by the operational plan of the General Staff which had been prepared in the event of a two-front war and which ran diametrically counter to Bethmann's political conceptions.

The Schlieffen plan which the younger Moltke rigidly adhered to (revised only in military-technical details) affected not in the first instance that Power which according to the bluff theory should be forced to back down (i.e. Russia) but provoked the Power with whom Bethmann hoped to reach an agreement, namely Britain, by requiring that German troops march through Belgium to whom Britain was committed. So the diplomatic front of the *Entente* which had been loosened by the Chancellor's efforts was immediately retightened as soon as the pressure of the German military during the crisis became evident.[39] As Gerhard Ritter had so passionately pointed out, the civilian leadership was crippled by the requirements of the generals; diplomacy was torpedoed by alleged strategic necessity.[40]

[38] Ibid., p. 343.
[39] Ibid.
[40] c.f. Gerhard Ritter, *Staatskunst und Kriegshandwerk*, II, p. 329.

38 THE POLITICS OF ILLUSION

Bethmann had accepted the claims of the generals who were concerned that their plan must be given every chance of success, but in giving it that priority the chance for the success of Bethmann's own risk-policy of calculated bluff was reduced to a minimum. Either the *Entente* backed down on all fronts or there would be the great general war without the peripheral conflicts of the smaller "satellite" or representative states as in the previous Balkan wars. These were the alternatives to which the whole crisis had been reduced.[41] But in the Riezler–Bethmann scheme of things there was still one slim possibility, after the war broke out, of it being terminated before it took on wider proportions. This would have been a function of that universal fear of a revolutionary post-war situation which would be induced by trying to fight the war until the point of complete exhaustion and ruin of one side. Such a prolonged war would have strong repercussions in the wider populations of the other belligerents and so the governments concerned would have every interest in keeping the war short. This, of course, was the illusion which Bethmann cultivated after the original bluff concept of diplomacy had broken down.

It remains now to summarise Hillgruber's analysis of Bethmann's actions at the beginning and at the outcome of the July–August crisis. Applying the Riezler concept to Bethmann it can be argued that he regarded the assassination of Franz Ferdinand in Sarajevo as probably the last chance in a deteriorating situation, by means of an Austro-Hungarian action against Serbia, to achieve a readjustment of the power relationships in the Balkans in favour of Austria-Hungary, but only to an extent which could just be accepted by Russia. It was reasoned that although this would affect the latter's prestige, it did not affect her vital interests. In any case, the decision whether or not to make it into an issue of war between Great Powers would rest with Russia. Bethmann initiated the policy of the calculated risk with his "blank cheque" to Vienna and thereby assigned to Austria-Hungary a particular role which she did not fully understand. The intention was that by swift Austro-Hungarian

41 Hillgruber, "Riezlers Theorie", p. 343.

action against Serbia, Russian Balkan policy would suffer a reverse and thus Austria-Hungary would have thereby given a boost to her waning prestige as Great Power. This would have presented the world with an accomplished fact and the ensuing crisis could be settled through diplomatic negotiations with the *Entente*. Riezler's diary of 8 July contains the following entry: *"fait accompli* and then friendly towards the *Entente,* the shock can be endured".[42]

Hillgruber is of the opinion that Bethmann saw some, though limited, chance of success in this procedure if Vienna acted quickly; less chance if Vienna procrastinated. Bethmann himself recorded in his memoirs that Germany virtually had to take this action (i.e. support Austria-Hungary) because it was in Germany's vital interests to see that the Danube monarchy did not collapse since this would have made the Reich hopelessly dependent upon Russia. Such a capitulation would have been intolerable and tantamount to self-emasculation (*Selbstentmannung*).[43]

The Chancellor seemed at the time (5–6 July) to have envisaged two alternatives: either to exploit the minimal chance and confront the risk, or to capitulate in the face of a general European trend which threatened to lead to Germany's complete isolation. Just how great Bethmann saw the risk he chose to confront is documented in the Riezler diary of 7 July: "An action against Serbia can lead to world war" — the result of over-bluffing. But on 8 July he seems to have become more sanguine: "If the war does not come, if the Czar does not want it, or France, thoroughly bewildered, counsels peace, then we still have prospects of breaking up the *Entente* through this action."[44] Other grounds spoke for adopting this forward course. Riezler noted Bethmann's views on the evening of 6 July, i.e. after the sending of the "blank cheque":

> The *Entente* knew that Germany was fully crippled. Austria was becoming weaker and weaker and ever less mobile. The military

[42] Ibid., p. 346.
[43] Ibid., pp. 346–7. c.f. Stern, "Bethmann Hollweg", p. 267.
[44] Ibid., p. 347. c.f. Stern, "Bethmann Hollweg", p. 264.

power of Russia was growing rapidly. The intelligence on the
Anglo-Russian naval talks gave serious cause to reckon with an
English landing attempt in Pommerania . . . If Germany failed to
stand behind Austria-Hungary, then the latter would approach the
Western Powers whose arms were open and we lose the last
military ally.[45]

It appears that the decisive point for Bethmann was "Russia's
ever growing demands and her colossal explosive power".[46]
Indeed, Bethmann saw Russia as the towering threat which in
a few years could be warded off.[47]

Although it soon became evident that Austria-Hungary was
not capable of mounting the swift action envisaged by Bethmann
so that a pre-requisite for the success of his scheme was lost,
he nevertheless stood by his original decision because now more
than before the only alternative was complete capitulation. He
therefore rejected any mediation attempts by Britain until the
Austrian action should record a success against Serbia and
insisted, despite many warning voices, that the localised war
must take place. And in this he accepted that the Austro-
Hungarian advance in the south be fully carried out even
though in the event of Russian armed intervention it would have
presented considerable military difficulties to transport these
troops into action against Russia; a fact which would jeopardise
the success of the previously settled arrangements of the Austro-
Hungarian and German General Staffs.[48]

Only on 29 July (i.e. on the second day of the Austro-
Serbian war) was Bethmann convinced that after the first
Austrian action against Serbia on one hand and after the
arrival of disquietening news of Russian military preparations
on the other, the point had been reached where the escalation
of the crisis could be stopped and the diplomatic negotiations
which Britain was pressing would have to begin — particularly
in view of the fact that Britain appeared to agree that Austria
might occupy parts of Serbia as a basis for a future arrangement.[49] However, in the meantime Bethmann had begun to
doubt the possibility of a rational steering of events.

[45] Ibid., p. 348.   [46] Ibid., c.f. Stern, "Bethmann Hollweg", p. 266.
[47] Ibid.
[48] Ibid. c.f. L. C. F. Turner, *Origins of the First World War*, p. 8.
[49] Ibid., p. 349.

Already on 20 July, Riezler noted that his mood was serious, "the Chancellor resolute and silent". A week later he recorded that Bethmann "sees doom (*Fatum*) greater than human power hanging over Europe and our own people", but added the same day, "he is entirely changed, he has no time to brood, and is therefore fresh, active, and lively without disquiet".[50]

Fritz Stern comments that "the juxtaposition of fatalism and energy is not odd or unusual: Calvinists, too, believe in predestination and act decisively".[51] Only the very serious news of 29 July caused Bethmann to make an attempt to halt the gathering crisis and to achieve some arrangement on the basis of the *status quo*. But Bethmann's room for manoeuvre had already been reduced to a depressing minimum; the first news of Russian mobilisation meant that the *de facto* leadership of Germany passed as it were imperceptibly to the generals who, as stated above, were anxious about the execution of their prearranged plan. Military-strategic considerations had a clear priority over the further pursuance of Bethmann's political strategy which, of course, lost its basis because of the military need to march through Belgium. German diplomacy was then relegated to the ancillary role of smoke-screening German military planning. A further contributing factor in the collapse of Bethmann's conception was the impossibility of getting Vienna, once having been urged to energetic military action, now abruptly to turn about face and adopt a conciliatory and diplomatic attitude within the concert of the Powers, i.e. to interrupt suddenly the attack only just begun and accept the British mediation which the Germans until this point had intentionally frustrated.[52]

On 30 July Bethmann confessed at a session of the Prussian Ministry of State, "that all governments including Russia's – and the large majority of the peoples were really peaceful but the direction had been lost and the stone had begun to roll".[53] The great European war which, as a result of the German operational plan, engaged all five Great Powers simultaneously,

[50] Stern, "Bethmann Hollweg", p. 266.   [51] Ibid.
[52] Hillgruber, "Riezlers Theorie", p. 349.   [53] Ibid., p. 350.

could no longer be held within limits by any desperate manoeuvre of German diplomacy which was now functioning totally
in the service of military strategy. Instead of an attempt to guide
the crisis on a rational basis Bethmann was forced to make a
"leap in the dark".[54]

When reading this reconstruction of the crisis by Andreas
Hillgruber one is impressed above all by the mutual inter-
dependence of historians, i.e. by the fact that such an analysis
was only made possible by many historians reflecting on the
theme from many different angles.

In a sense it was all triggered off by Fritz Fischer's revision
where he emphasised the power structure of the Wilhelmine
state and of the peculiar tendencies, ideologies and tensions
within it. Then, because Gerhard Ritter believed this approach
was unjust to the person of Bethmann Hollweg, he presented a
sympathetic apologia for the Chancellor's actions, seeing him
trapped in an insoluble dilemma. Again, this view led to
Hillgruber's more detailed "ideological" explanation which was
only made possible by the publication of extracts of Riezler's
diary by K. D. Erdmann, which must have suggested to
Hillgruber the need to examine whether there was any consist-
ency between Bethmann's actions in the crisis and the world-
political ideas of his chief consultant which had already been
published before the war.

All these analyses are extremely valuable; they indicate the
complexity of arriving at historical "truth". Everything must
be stated with qualifications. No one can impute to the Chancellor of the German Reich in 1914 the same motives which
determined Adolf Hitler's war aims in 1939. However, it
must be observed that the Chancellor was imprisoned in an
anachronistic world of ideas which made the war possible; and
these ideas emerged from a gloomy, fatalist, irrational background which Hillgruber states was a common feature of
intellectual life in the Wilhelmine era.[55] It was against this that
the Riezler-Bethmann quasi-rational attempt was made during

[54] Ibid.

[*for footnote 55 see p.* 43]

the period of the great arms race to exploit international crises for the extension of limited power political goals.

Finally, one cannot escape the observation that the understanding of world politics by the German leadership in 1914 was the product of generations of a peculiarly German conception of the nation's history. In short, Germans had been educated in a power-state ideology which consciously rejected enlightened, liberal, cosmopolitan and democratic concepts as being alien to the German spirit, and instead persisted in cultivating anachronistic conservative, feudal and militarist values which regarded war as an instrument of progress.

This system was in fact the construction of Prusso-German historians and philosophers over the previous century. The end product was Neo-Rankeanism which was nothing more or less than the ideology of *Weltpolitik*. And it is because Fischer's work constitutes the most radical departure hitherto from this entire system that there is a crisis in German historiography today.[56] By ruthlessly discarding the ideological encumbrances

[55] Ibid., pp. 350–351. Note that the reviewer in the *Times Literary Supplement* (31 August 1973, p. 1006) of Konrad Jarausch's *The Enigmatic Chancellor* described Bethmann rather aptly as a chaplain on a pirate ship. "It is the pirates that matter, not their chaplain's vague pangs of conscience."

[56] The way in which German historians conceived of the state is an interesting example of how a group of scholars over a long period were committed to the same set of concepts and assumptions. To use Thomas S. Kuhn's phrase, these were the paradigms of the "scientific community". In other words, the German historians and the educated élite accepted unquestioningly as scientifically valid the notions about the nature of the state which had been deposited by seminal thinkers such as Herder, Hegel, and Ranke over a period of more than a century. Although, as has been pointed out, there had been earlier significant opponents to the paradigm of beliefs represented by these German scholars, it was left to Fritz Fischer to effect the final break down of that paradigm and pave the way for a new role for the historical discipline in Germany. The relevance of Kuhn's book, *The Structure of Scientific Revolutions* to a problem such as we have here is very great. The basic concept that bodies of knowledge in an educated community are propagated in the form of accepted paradigms seems to be borne

[*footnote continued on p.* 44]

of the past, Fischer has not only paved the way for a more objective historiography in Germany, he has taken an all-important step in "democratising" the historical discipline (i.e. by rejecting the basic conservative, state-veneration of his predecessors) and therewith will democratise the political values of future generations of German students. Indeed, there can be no historiography without ideological commitment.

out in the case of the German historians very well indeed. Here, Fritz Fischer has wrought a "scientific revolution". Recognition of this is being made frequently in Germany in references to Fischer's work. Most recently, Werner Hornung has written that Fischer by virtue of the controversy which he unleashed had contributed more than any other post-war historian to forcing a revision of the assumptions upon which he and his colleagues had formerly based their work. Fischer's pupils and those stimulated by him have begun to give German historical scholarship a new theoretical framework. See Werner Hornung, "Geschichte als Sozialwissenschaft—Nachhilfe für Historiker", *Die Zeit*, Nr. 45, 2 November 1973, p. 27.

"Yet the truest friends of Germany are those who reveal her true foe to her; and the new Germany's true foe is the old Germany."

HERMANN KANTOROWICZ,
*The Spirit of British Policy and the
Myth of the Encirclement of Germany*
(1929), p. 20

PART TWO
The War of Illusions

Introduction

Eight years after his epoch-making *Griff nach der Weltmacht* the now world famous Hamburg professor presented students of modern German history with yet another intensive piece of national self-examination. Having shocked his colleagues in 1961 not only with a ruthless exposé of Imperial Germany's expansionist aims in the Great War, but also by presenting a convincing thesis of Germany's chief responsibility for the outbreak of the war in August 1914, Fischer set out to underpin this by subjecting pre-war German policy from 1911 to 1914 to a detailed scrutiny. What resulted is a massive (783 pages) indictment of a style of government which based both domestic and foreign policy on dangerously irrational concepts, and these were shared by the entire "Nation". The war of 1914–18 was, therefore, not the result of a tragic diplomatic error but a conscious, if nervous calculation by a power-deluded state which believed her hour of destiny in world history had arrived.

This view was, understandably, angrily repudiated by most of Fischer's colleagues. For them the Bismarckian-Wilhelmine state was essentially a healthy political structure and it was mainly due to the jealousy and trickery of the other Powers combined with Germany's *Nibelungentreue* (loyalty to the death) to Austria-Hungary which brought about its tragic collapse. Again, understandably, the chief role of these historians after 1945 had been that of apologists for the Wilhelmine Reich, explaining the Third Reich as a *Betriebsunfall* (an accident in the works). This is to suggest that Hitlerism was exclusively the product of the anti-Versailles movement in Germany and hence had no roots in German developments prior to 1919.[1]

Because Fischer has had both the courage and insight to depart from this line, we have the crisis in German historiography referred to above.[2] Stubborn opponents of Fischer's radical revision had initiated a virtual *Methodenstreit* but which on closer scrutiny was essentially an attempt to discredit a scholarly work simply because its conclusions were found by many to be politically unpalatable. The basic argument was that Fischer had a preconceived thesis and selected only those sources which supported that thesis. This view is quite untenable since Fischer and his assistants have not only done a more complete investigation of the documents than anyone else, they have also had to confront the counter-arguments of many weighty critics. These have all been taken into account and refuted on a scholarly basis. Even Fischer's most persistent opponents such as Gerhard Ritter (1888–1967) and Golo Mann, for example, were forced to agree with him that Imperial Germany's policies unleashed the war; however, they imputed to Germany's leaders defensive rather than offensive motives.[3]

In the case of Gerhard Ritter, for example, one's assessment of the real nature of German policy will be determined by the

[1] See my paper "Hitler between Prussianism and Mass Hysteria—Some Post-War German Views", *Historical Journal* (University of Newcastle, N.S.W., Australia) 1974, and Manfred Schlenke, "Das 'preussische Beispiel' in Propaganda und Politik des Nationalsozialismus", *APZ* B27/68, 3 July 1968.

[2] Fritz Fischer, *Krieg der Illusionen*, p. 12. J. C. G. Röhl has commented recently on Fischer's work by stating that "the publication of his monumental study of Germany's aims in the First World War in 1961 aroused the greatest storm the German historical world has ever seen. Despite the initial outcry, his basic conclusions have now been widely accepted and his influence is clearly discernible in most of the monographs now appearing in Germany. Something of a historiographical revolution has occurred." (*From Bismarck to Hitler*, p. xii).

[3] For a more detailed analysis of Fischer's chief critics see the present writer's *The War Aims of Imperial Germany: Professor Fritz Fischer and His Critics*, Brisbane 1968.

extent to which one is willing to absolve Bethmann Hollweg from the charge of either having lost control of policy-making to the military leadership against his better·judgment, or of being blindly incapable of assessing the nature of the crisis which Germany forced in July–August 1914. For Golo Mann it is simply that Germany was not the only "beast of prey" in the international jungle. He seems to consider that in all the Powers there resided the same aggressive drives and ruthless will to expansion at the cost of weaker powers. For this reason it was wrong and unhistorical of Fischer to highlight these drives and this ruthless will in one Power of the time in isolation from the others. Fischer's tacit reply to this latter charge is simply that it is precisely this analysis of the unique structure and tendencies within the Wilhelmine empire which is needed in order for the German people in particular to be able to understand their country's past, and by implication, the present. It will not do simply to suggest that all Great Powers harbour essentially the same brutal energies and lusts; the historian is obliged to determine where possible the unique characteristics of a particular historical phenomenon. It is somewhat ironical that Fischer has been taken to task for trying to do just this. Indeed, there are many inconsistencies in the criticisms levelled at him. The late Gerhard Ritter, perhaps Fischer's most passionate critic, assigned to the historian the role of reflecting on the national past with a view to discerning the "right" direction for the future. It would appear to the non-German observer that Fischer is actually doing this but his method was wrong, according to Ritter, since Fischer repudiated a great deal of the legacy of the past. Ritter, on the other hand, had been at pains to retain much of the political legacy of the Bismarckian-Wilhelmine era in a conservative effort to absolve then existing institutions from any suggestion that they could have adumbrated the Third Reich. Ritter strenuously rejected the idea that Hitler and the forces which carried the Third Reich were the products of ideals and aims generated in Germany before 1914.

It is in fact the aim of Fischer's second book to present an exhaustive analysis of pre-1914 German policy. He was particularly stimulated to do this not only because he promised the academic world this study when he published his "first book" in 1961 but also because of the need to refute critics of that work who maintained that Germany's policy in 1914–18 was only to be understood as a reaction to the *Entente* policies and that before 1914 there was no German programme for expansion. Indeed, there were those who even denied the existence of an official German imperialism before 1914 and who tried to attribute any expression of this to the fanatical "Pan Germans" who were, after all, only a type of "lunatic fringe". Others, such as Gerhard Ritter, were satisfied to talk about war aims as merely the wish-dreams of patriotic Germans who had no real effect on the formulation of policy. Fischer has shown that such views are no longer tenable. In revealing what he calls the "self-understanding" of the social groups which supported the Imperial German Government Fischer has presented new insights into the character of German policy and the peculiar nature of the power structure of the Reich.

Naturally, Fischer recognises certain common traits among the Great Powers of the time but warns against compressing them all into a model which would fail to assess the variety of historical factors and "which would attempt to force the historical process into a Procrustian bed of sociological and politological categories".[4] There has to be a separate study for Germany (as, indeed, for all states) because from the 1880's onwards a peculiar development took place there which lent the country an impatient restlessness; as Fischer says, the tension between the old monarchical-feudal and bourgeois-commercial structure within the rapidly growing industrial state had never quite been reconciled. Here the social problem continued to exist unsolved in all its acerbity under the pressure of the alliance between Junkerdom and heavy industry; and further, Germany had entered the age of *Weltpolitik* and world commerce at a relatively unfavourable point in time, namely when the world was already to a large extent divided up among the

[4] Fischer, *Krieg . . .* , p. 12.

established Great Powers. All this provided a unique climate for the growth of a peculiar type of nationalism and imperialism within the young German nation. Further, in demonstrating the close connection between economic growth and imperialistic ambitions, Fischer claims to have made a contribution to the history of the continuity in German political and social development from the later Bismarck period onwards.

Fischer discerns, especially from the international crisis of 1905–06 and at the latest from that of 1911, an intensification of this process; there were increased imperialistic claims resulting from Germany's economic upsurge. Therein developed the forces of a new popular nationalism which threatened to burst the structure of the old bureaucratic state (*Obrigkeitsstaat*). Further, Fischer believes he can show that the interrelationship between the economy and politics was no retrospectively constructed hypothesis, but rather it was a factor which "quite essentially" contributed to determining diplomatic action as well as tendencies within domestic politics. He wants also to show that certain social groups forced decisions which apologists would have preferred to attribute to the upper echelons of the bureaucracy which was supposed to be "above group interests".

The question opened here is that of the social basis of the government and the monarchy. This was mirrored in the debate concerning the parliamentarising and democratising of the constitution which was very evident from 1912 at the latest, during the Chancellorship of Bethmann Hollweg. His own slogan about trying to pursue a "policy of diagonals" indicates that the government was not able to reach its decisions in a vacuum but rather that it had to consider concrete social factors and power relationships.

Here Fischer strikes at the neuralgic point of German historiography, namely the question regarding the "primacy of foreign policy" over domestic policy. He sees, on the contrary, foreign policy being determined by urgent domestic questions. In this case a successful imperialistic foreign policy was supposed to secure the position of the ruling classes; indeed, it was hoped that the increased social tensions within Germany could have been overcome by a war. Thereby the masses, hitherto alienated from the Reich, would be won over and integrated into that monarchist system. Fischer observes that warnings by Bethmann Hollweg who foresaw the need for democratisation as a result of the war — a process which he himself did not desire — only confirm how widespread such ideas really were. In any case the domestic political crisis had become manifest by 1912. The decision to go to war in 1914 was, besides these domestic political motives, chiefly determined by military considerations which for their part depended upon economic and power-political goals. All these factors — with regard to the masses as well as to the Kaiser and other factors of psychological nature — had to be taken into the government's calculation. If all these forces are surveyed one can recognise a clear continuity of aims between the pre-war period and throughout the war.

Summing up his thesis, Fischer asserts that the same dynamism together with its domestic political components which caused the leadership in 1897 to embark on a "world policy" remained effective without a break until 1914. In the late 'nineties the hope and goal was a "Greater Germany" and the preservation of the conservative system. The illusions of this conception of 1897 led to the illusions of 1914.

This is Fischer's view as stated in his foreword; the book itself is a weighty documentation of this position which has been criticised as resembling a crown prosecutor's indictment rather than narrative history.[5]

[5] Rudolf Augstein, "Deutschlands Fahne auf dem Bosporus", *Der Spiegel,* 24 November 1969, p. 87. c.f. Karl Heinz Janssen, "Das Spiel mit dem Krieg", *Die Zeit,* 17 October 1969, p. 74.

CHAPTER I

The War of Illusions—The Historiographical Assumptions

They brought history into touch with the nation's life, and gave it an influence it had never possessed out of France; and they won for themselves the making of opinions mightier than laws.

LORD ACTON,
"German Schools of History",
EHR I (1886), p. 32

Methodologically, Fischer's "second book" has been judged to be very much traditional German historiography by certain reviewers.[1] It is of course true that the author and his assistants were all trained in the prevailing German school of historicism and certainly the book reveals many characteristics of that tradition. An essential feature of this was the striving after "objectivity" which meant seeking to depict individuals and institutions of the past in their own context and on their own terms strictly avoiding the application of norms of judgment from the present. One was at pains to establish the *Selbstverständnis* of individual historical phenomena. This approach placed great emphasis on the painstaking construction of the broadest possible basis of relevant sources and the employment of a predominantly descriptive method. In this regard, neither *Griff nach der Weltmacht* nor *Krieg der Illusionen* represents works of a methodological pioneering nature.[2] Fischer's in-

[1] c.f. Georg G. Iggers, *Deutsche Geschichtswissenschaft*, pp. 359–360, and Volker R. Berghahn, "Fritz Fischer und seine Schüler", pp. 147–148.

[2] c.f. Arnold Sywottek, "Die Fischer Kontroverse . . . ", pp. 21–36. Here the writer seeks to explain how Fischer was motivated to begin

[*footnote 2 continued on p.* 54]

debtedness is still more to Leopold von Ranke than to Karl Marx, though the indebtedness to both is very evident. Perhaps because of this Fischer's work exhibits certain features which mark it as revolutionary within the context of German historiography. First and foremost it is the author's attitutde to the German state which signifies a major departure from that usually revealed by established German historians. Fischer's work is inspired by a spirit of ruthless national self-examination and a consistent determination not to overlook any "uncomfortable" details, i.e. facts which tend to besmirch the national image. Hermann Kantorowicz observed that continental historians tended to write in the service of national policy and the German historicists had always done this.[3] Fischer's works condemn rather than praise German policy.

The corollary to this feature is again quite revolutionary. The state (in this case the Wilhelmine Empire) is not regarded as sacrosanct in the Hegelian-Rankean sense. Indeed, if there was any aura of the World Spirit about the Bismarckian state structure, Fischer and his students have dispelled it in the mind of German conservatives once and for all. Any nostalgia for *Opas Monarchie* (Grandad's monarchy), as Imanuel Geiss recently commented, has been irrevocably destroyed.[4] And this is essentially "what the fuss has been about" regarding Fischer's books.[5] He and Geiss have exposed the interior flaws of his research. Fischer had recognised the need for a comprehensive study of German war aims in the First World War based on all the primary German sources and had proceeded to go about researching it in the traditional way. He had wanted merely to analyse and depict the formation of political will which led to the ripening of German war aims (pp. 32–33).

[3] Hermann Kantorowicz, *The Spirit of British Policy* . . . , p. 20, and Antoine Guilland, *Modern Germany and her Historians*, pp. 10–11.

[4] In a radio talk from the Norddeutscher Rundfunk (1 February 1970 —First Programme from 18.45 to 19.00 hours) entitled "Geschichte and Geschichtswissenschaft" in the series *Gedanken zur Zeit*. See also Professor Geiss's epilogue to Emil Ludwig, *Wilhelm der Zweite*, pp. 307–315.

[5] The phrase is by the author of a review article on books about Germany and the First World War entitled "War Heroes", *Times Literary Supplement*, 31 August 1973, p. 1006.

Wilhelmine Germany to the intense embarrassment of those older generation historians who had drawn inspiration from it and had even worn the Kaiser's uniform. They had passionately believed in the rightness of the German cause in 1914–1918 and were understandably shocked and dismayed by Fischer's revelations.[6] Conversely the post-1945 generation of historians have in general been able to endorse Fischer's characterisation of the Wilhelmine epoch.

An additional "revolutionary" aspect of Fischer's work has been noted by Wolfgang J. Mommsen who identifies a moralistic quality in it. Indeed, he has labelled Fischer and his school as the *gesinnungsethische*.[7] This is to suggest that Fischer and Geiss in particular approach their subject as crusading democrats who in drawing attention in the way they do to the nationalistic, bellicose and anti-democratic attitudes, values and ideals which characterised the Wilhelmine era are in fact condemning them. And this moralistic tone is a further departure from traditional historicism, a central tenet of which was to understand (*verstehen*) rather than to judge past epochs. However, this feature alone is insufficient reason for the vehemence of the anti-Fischer criticism among his colleagues. The high degree of acrimony in the debate can hardly be explained by their rejection of a narrative style because it offended their aesthetic sensibilities. Rather, the emotion-laden response to Fischer's work is due to the fact that he has probed none too delicately at a number of so-called "neuralgic points" or taboos in the German historiographical self-image. And the reaction has been all the more neurotic in some cases because Fischer as a long established member of the *Historiker Zunft* (i.e. the guild of German history professors) has in a real sense turned "heretic" towards the beliefs shared by that august body of scholars. Until Fischer came along in 1961 with his iconoclastic thesis regarding the expansionist nature of German war-aims

[6] c.f. Geiss, "Westdeutsche Geschichtswissenschaft seit 1945", pp. 441–445.

[7] Wolfgang J. Mommsen, "Domestic Factors in German Foreign Policy before 1914", *CEH*, VI (1973), p. 8.

in 1914–1918, the war guilt issue and the Hitler problem had been neatly disposed of in the consciousness of historians. The renegade Fischer, as V. R. Berghahn observed, then ruthlessly smashed up the painstakingly constructed explanation of the outbreak of the First World War and the rise of Adolf Hitler.[8]

This explanation was based on the assumption that the German Reich had been snared in a sinister plot of encircle-ment by the Triple Entente and had only gone to war in 1914 to protect her own interests. When in 1919, with the humiliating defeat, the infamous Versailles Treaty imposed the war-guilt accusation upon Germany coupled with the burden of repara-tions, the German people were thrown into confusion, despair and misery. It was then not surprising that after the political and economic chaos of the Weimar period, they elected to office the one man who was the most vigorous opponent of Versailles. They could not be blamed for failing to predict that Hitler was a demon who would lead them again to an even greater catastrophe. This was the *fate* of the German nation and not her *guilt*.

Such a train of logic was represented by most conservative historians in post-1945 Germany. Chief among these was Gerhard Ritter who quickly emerged as Fischer's doughtiest opponent.[9] As perhaps the most eloquent apologist for Wilhel-mine Germany he preferred to speak of *mysterious forces* and *demons* which had disrupted the otherwise healthy course of modern German history. Professor Fischer and his school have shown that it was not supernatural forces of evil which were determining events but men of flesh, blood and passions.[10] By demonstrating who conceived what policies and how they were carried out, Fischer has once and for all exploded the "myth of encirclement" (a task attempted already in 1929 by Hermann Kantorowicz but whose prophetic warnings fell on

[8] Berghahn, "Fritz Fischer und seine Schüler", pp. 145–146.

[9] For a summary of Ritter's position, see the present writer's *The War Aims of Imperial Germany: Professor Fritz Fischer and his Critics*, pp. 220–222, as well as his "The July Crisis 1914: Historiography and Weltanschauung" in *Questioning the Past*, ed. D. P. Crook, pp. 322–335.

[10] Berghahn, "Fritz Fischer und seine Schüler", p. 146.

deac ears).[11] Now, however, Fischer has not only debunked the encirclement myth but also the myth of German war "innocence". In addition he has pointed to the continuity between Imperial German and Nazi war aims. This is a further sense in which Fischer's work is revolutionary. Germans have now been forced to revise their image of Bismarckian-Wilhelmine Germany and abandon their residual veneration for the conservative, monarchical and nationalistic values and attitudes of that epoch because these foreshadowed the Nazi era. In doing so they have also been compelled to reflect on the basis of their current political attitudes.

It is in this last respect that Fischer's work is what the Germans call a *Politikum* of a particularly efficacious kind. That is to say, the book has had profound political implications. While there cannot now be a restoration of the borders of the Bismarckian Empire simply because of the Cold War power constellation in Europe, neither can there be any revival of historically based claims for its restoration. The moral basis for such claims has been totally exploded by the Fischer school.[12] If their work represents a change in the historical-political consciousness of a scholarly élite, the impact of it upon the student population must also effect a change of consciousness. This theme will be taken up in the final chapter.

Turning to *War of Illusions* the student is confronted with a massive study which seeks to explain the aggressive thrusts of German foreign policy, especially from 1911 to 1914 by examining the interaction of domestic social and political problems with the nation's external situation. As Fischer himself has noted, this approach was a departure from the traditional stress on foreign policy by historians of the Ranke school who regarded the latter's principle of the "primacy of foreign policy" as immutable. This meant that everything in the state was subordinated to the demands of foreign policy. What Fischer has shown is precisely the opposite situation. It was rather the

---

[11] Hermann Kantorowicz, *The Spirit of British Policy and the Myth of the Encirclement.*

[12] Geiss, *Studien über Geschichte* . . . , pp. 195–197.

demands of domestic policy which moulded the character of
Germany's foreign policy. In short, it was ultimately the determination of the German power elite to resist all social-
political and constitutional changes within the Reich which had
led to the adoption of a forward, erratic and aggressive foreign
policy.

The image of Wilhelmine Germany which emerges in
Fischer's work is that of a rigidly hierarchical, bureaucratised,
anti-democratic and self-consciously nationalistic social order
which was resisting at every turn all demands to modernise the
constitution and to make rational concessions to the forces of
social democracy. The inner tensions which inevitably developed
in a country where the largest single party (by 1912) was excluded for ever from participation in political decision-making
found their solution in the provocation of external tensions.

Fischer's account begins with an investigation of the transformation of Germany from an agricultural to an industrial
society. The purpose is to sketch in the socio-economic framework within which Germany assumed her political posture.
Already under Bismarck Germany's dilemma as a developing
industrial state was becoming obvious. Her choice was between
maintaining free-trade or adopting a protectionist policy with
a view to exploiting the vast Central European market. By the
1890's the choice had been clearly taken for the latter. This,
Fischer asserts, was due to the then prevailing belief that
Germany would have to compete against the so-called "three
world empires" of Britain, Russia and the United States of
America.[13] Indeed, by the mid-1890's Germany's vigorous
economic growth nurtured the belief that she was about to
outstrip Britain and become an equal partner among the Great
Powers. So it was the domestic factors of a hot-house industrial
growth, the socio-economic alliance between Junkerdom and
the *nouveaux riches* industrialists with their common hostility
towards social democracy which determined the stance of
German imperialism. This was made even more pugnacious by
the conviction of economists and historians that Germany had

[13] Fischer, *Krieg der Illusionen*, p. 24.

an historic mission to compete with the existing three "world empires".

This complex of factors contained several extremely dangerous components. First, there was the uncompromising attitude on the part of industrialists towards the workers and their political aspirations. Trade unionism and socialism were looked upon as the chief enemy of the socio-political order to be suppressed at all costs. If there was one factor which united all the other parties in the *Reichstag* it was their common hostility towards the growing Social Democratic Party.[14] The relevance of this aspect of domestic politics was very great because it seduced the ruling élite into regarding war as a means of uniting the nation as well as providing an excuse for eliminating a large professed anti-monarchist and pacifist element in national life. Indeed, war would achieve overall social and political integration.

The second dangerous component was the idea of the nation's character and destiny in the mind of the educated classes. This had been moulded by the memory of Prussia's three short wars which led to the unification of Germany and the Reich's subsequent role as arbitrator of Europe during the Congress of Berlin in 1878. All this provided the basis for a peculiar national pride sustained by an unshakeable faith in Prusso-German military superiority which led to a cult of militarism and the longing for power, prestige and further successes. Indeed, the Prussianisation of Germany in 1871 had created an anti-democratic, militarist, authoritarian state which rejected not only the political legacy of the Enlightenment but also the German experience of 1848.

If this were not enough, a third factor emerged which increased the Germans' predisposition for resorting to military solutions to real or imagined political problems. Fischer explains this as the result of a so-called cultural pessimism which emerged concomitantly with the spread of industrialisation and capitalism in Germany. It was expressed in the paradoxical rejection of the profit motive as well as of political and economic

[14] Ibid., pp. 47 and 53.

liberalism — paradoxical because Germany was experiencing a boom under capitalism and was jubilant at her achievements. But all this was at the price of a bad conscience. And here, claims Fischer, lies the motive for the contemptuous repudiation of the cosmopolitanism and pacifist tendencies of the West. It was this state of mind which produced the remarkable wartime book by Werner Sombart, *Händler und Helden* (1915) (i.e. Traders and Heroes) in which the shallow, frivolous, sporting, commercial spirit of the English was contrasted with the manly, serious and honourable German spirit which had its roots in the ideals of medieval knighthood and chivalry.

These components determined the posture of Wilhelmine Germany. Out of this socio-economic and intellectual historical mould emerged German policy from Bismarck to Bethmann Hollweg. Fischer's detailed documentation of this complex of domestic and foreign policy which takes account of intellectual-historical as well as socio-economic factors is a mighty *tour de force* which, because of the immense accumulation of data alone, represents a work of monumental importance.

II

In order to appreciate Fischer's significance in the history of historical writing it is important to enquire what he believed he was doing. What is Fischer's own conception of the historian's task and method?[15] He stresses that he was trained in the "school" which Leopold von Ranke firmly established in Germany. However, Fischer notes, as this school developed into the second half of the nineteenth century, the broad universalist and humanist quality of Ranke's historiography had become narrowed. Inspired more by the romanticism which infused the German national movement, German historiography concentrated on the emerging German nation-state with an emphasis on diplomacy and European power politics.

[15] Fritz Fischer, "Aufgaben und Methoden der Geschichtswissenschaft" in *Geschichtsschreibung—Epochen, Methoden, Gestaltung,* ed. Jürgen Scheskewitz, pp. 7–28.

Fischer recalls that after the foundation of the Bismarckian Reich there flourished an historical interest in constitutional and legal developments as well as in the achievements of the state in the spheres of civil administration, defence, the fiscal sector and welfare. Above all, it was Hegel's conceptions which dominated constitutional and historical thought in German universities. The state was regarded as a higher entity, the custodians of which were the jurists. Naturally this entity stood above the sordid conflict of forces within society itself. The latter with its various class and economic interests, with its concern for "filthy lucre", with the profit motive and the problems of production did not command the central interest of the German historian. At best, these socio-economic factors were dealt with in appendices to works devoted to the history of states and their heroes.

Fischer observes that a major reason for this one-sidedness in German historiography was that many German historians were either the sons of pastors or classical scholars for whom the world of affairs, of industry and commerce was relatively unknown territory. Furthermore, as university professors these men were state officials who saw themselves as defenders rather than critics of the existing political order which was monarchist-authoritarian. This became clear whenever they were required to make historical judgments about the great issues of politics, i.e. war and peace, revolution and social upheaval. Indeed, so deeply rooted were German historians in this tradition that they retained many of these attitudes of mind even after the monarchy had disappeared, i.e. during the nineteen-twenties. In this way they sustained a specifically German "tradition of the state" into a period when an entirely new and liberalised view would have been more conducive to political stability.

In his survey of these developments Fischer has taken care to point out that the Hegelian-Rankean tradition was not entirely left unchallenged in Germany even before 1914. The famous *Methodenstreit* which Karl Lamprecht ignited at the turn of the century indicated that some established history professors were susceptible to influences from other sources such as Marx. However, Lamprecht's doctrine of "scientific history" which gave priority to what he called *Kulturgeschichte* provoked a vehement reaction from his "statist" colleagues who believed that history must concentrate on the nation alone and not seek to identify general laws about the growth of civilization. Other challenges to the traditional Hegelian-Rankean school were mounted by Max Weber and Otto Hintze but these made scarcely any noticeable impact on the prevailing methodological assumptions, even during the Weimar period.[16]

The chief reason for this, notes Fischer, was the general historical-political interest both before and after the First World War in the Olympian personality of Bismarck who was looked upon as a towering example for the lesser figures of the later Wilhelmine and the politically catastrophic Weimar period. An additional factor hindering the development of German historiography at that time was the general pre-occupation with the "war-guilt question" which consumed virtually the total energy of German as well as many non-German historians. This resulted in the inability of most German scholars to appreciate developments in social and economic history which were being made in France, Britain and the U.S.A. It was for this reason characteristic, wrote Fischer, that the only German historians of this epoch whose work was of pioneering quality in the field of social and economic factors in history had been exposed to influences in the U.S.A. These were G. W. F. Hallgarten and Eckart Kehr. Unfortunately, Hallgarten being Jewish had been forced to remain in the U.S.A., while Kehr had died in 1933, too young to have made an enduring impression. Then, of course, the deadening hand of the Third Reich stifled any further historiographical development.[17]

[16] See Bernhard vom Brocke's study, *Kurt Breysig—Geschichtswissenschaft zwischen Historismus und Soziologie.* Breysig (1866–1940) devoted his career to pioneering new methods in social sciences and history. He was closely allied to Max Weber and Otto Hintze, and was one of the first, and few, German scholars during the Wilhelmine era and the Weimar Republic consciously to depart from historicism to pioneer social history (p. 13).

[17] Fischer, "Aufgaben ₓ ₓ ₓ ", p. 16.

At this point Fischer makes the harrowingly frank observation that it was not purely scholarly reflection but rather the experience of the Nazi era which provided the decisive impetus for a radical revision of the traditional German historiographical assumptions. The historical events themselves, in particular Hitler's domestic and foreign policies, had to challenge the continued acceptance of the German idea of the *Rechtsstaat* as well as the traditional Machiavellian norms in the conduct of foreign policy.[18] As Fischer puts it, the Nazi dictatorship with its crimes on the domestic front coupled with the violence and lack of restraint in external affairs raised the inescapable question as to the extent to which German historical thinking had contributed to these things.

The German school had been all too inclined to explain the historical process in terms of the thoughts and deeds of the great personalities. And here Fischer touches upon the most vulnerable aspect of the historicist tradition, namely the tendency to get absorbed in the minutae of biography and in doing so to lose sight of the broader spectrum of the overall pattern of events. There was a resistance to the idea of applying the norms derived from natural law or Christianity to the course of history. The effect of this was that the individual actors in the historical drama were only described and "understood" but never criticised against any generally accepted norms of behaviour. In making this observation, Fischer is, of course, aware that the Western concept of natural law and morality, cannot be considered to have a transcendental character, but that concept of natural law itself is a result of the historical process, i.e. having emerged from the Judaic-Christian traditions, the Greek Polis, Roman Law and the ideas of human and civic rights as well as international law.[19]

[18] According to the definition given in *Der Grosse Brockhaus, Rechtsstaat* is a state in which the activity of the state is delimited by the "concept of the law", i.e. *Rechtsidee*. Within the framework of Hegelian historicism, the "law" must of course be inevitably biased towards the rights of the state as opposed to the rights of individual citizens as understood in the West.

[19] Fischer, "Aufgaben . . . ", p. 16.

With this clearly in mind Fischer has re-emphasised the Western Enlightenment tradition which most of his colleagues, in particular Gerhard Ritter had, with a pronounced defiance, repudiated. The experience of the Third Reich has demonstrated the grotesque absurdity of regarding the state as Hegel, Treitschke and even Meinecke had done as an entity standing above and beyond the demands of human morality. While recognising the universal insistence on national sovereignty and all that this implies for the relations between states, an unqualified submission to a Machiavellian-Hegelian view of the state which many German historians before the Nazi era had advocated, cannot any longer be tenable. If Fischer's work has any underlying concept, it is this. For traditional German historiography this conscious departure from the Hegelian-Rankean tradition is nothing short of revolutionary.

Having taken this step, Fischer now asks: What determines the relationship of the historian to the object of his enquiry? He recognises frankly that even when one has most sources available, it is still impossible either to establish beyond doubt the motives of the individual protagonists or even to assemble all relevant data. A further difficulty is to decide how one is to evaluate personalities against the supra-personal factors. No historian, admits Fischer, is able to illuminate equally all the details of the historical process even if they are categorised beyond doubt in their own period. So Fischer sees the historian confronted with the gigantic question as to what should command his chief attention. Is it the king, the statesmen, the captains of industry and commerce, the philosopher, the poet, the trade-union boss or party leader or even the electors? On the other hand, is it the socio-economic structure, the bureaucratic institutions or the various pressure groups? Is the historian concerned with individual personalities or the conditions under which the individual or individuals live(s)?

The German situation after 1945 saw the historical discipline exposed to the influences of the West as well as of Marxism as never before. The general result of this in West Germany had been a transfer of interest from the great personalities of history to a more balanced consideration of economic, social, institutional and intellectual factors. A commentator on this phenomenon, Werner Hornung, observed that until recently the German school of historians had been working in what he called "a methodological natural park" which had been isolated from the progressive developments of the outside world.[20] Fritz Fischer and his school have contributed more than any others to changing this situation in Germany. There are problems involved in this process and Fischer openly acknowledges them. Whereas previously the German historicist could proceed confidently applying his "strictly individualising method" leaving aside the structural factors, he is now faced with difficulties of evaluating the role of individuals as well as the totality of the historical process. Thereby he is confronted with a variety of categories instead of simply one generally accepted and established method. In addition to this he has the further problem of the connection between the process of recognition and his own subjective position to overcome.

Here Fischer shows himself to be an earnest and involved historian who is profoundly concerned with the validity of his scholarship. He recognises squarely that no matter how much the historian strives for objectivity he remains always a child of his times and is therefore unable to take up an observation point outside his own environment. However, adds Fischer, this is not only a limitation; it is also a fruitful impetus to the process of historical recognition. It is precisely the historian's subjectivity as a time-bound observer which for Fischer is the basis of the historian's interest in history simply because every epoch *requires* its historians to rewrite history. The more the historian is aware of his dependence upon the questions of his own time, nation and class formulated with reference to his own background, social position, education as well as his individual characteristics, the more he will be able to meet the demand to strive towards the highest possible objectivity. Fischer's stated goal is to let the individual historian's persona-

[20] Werner Hornung, "Geschichte als Sozialwissenschaft—Nachhilfe für Historiker", *Die Zeit*, Nr. 45, 2 November 1973, p. 27.

lity recede so that the object of his enquiry may emerge in sharper focus illuminated and set in its context. Any other approach would result in a tendentious historiography, particularly if the historian does not reflect on his own social and ideological position.

Further, maintains Fischer, the historian must be aware of the dual conditions imposed on his task: that concerning the ultimate object of enquiry and that concerning the historian's standpoint. It is in coming to grips with these issues that the principle of selection is raised. First, there is the question of the relation of the individual historian to his environment, and second, the question which of the great phenomena of historical life should command his attention. Should it be the state in its relationship to other states? Should it be the domestic factors of political life or the supra-national factors such as social structures, culture or quite generally human society?

In answering the first question, there are, according to Fischer, two possible extremes. One is the view that "men make history" so that one accepts that the totality of the historical process is contained in the biography of great men. While the contribution of "historical personalities" is undeniable, it is obviously inadequate to concentrate solely upon them. This is true since regardless of the greatness of individuals, limits are set to their actions within the social, economic, institutional, intellectual as well as international framework. Nevertheless, observes Fischer, beyond the simple reply, namely that the historian must seek to set the individual actors in their social context, there is the superordinate problem of determining which of the so-called objective conditions (the historical institutions, traditions, customs, the general social structure in their inter-connections and changes) is to be the prime object of enquiry. On the other hand, is it to be the virtues, vices, achievements and failures of the individual personality?

The Marxist position which sees the motor of history in the economic conditions, in the possession or non-possession of the means of production and in the class struggle is regarded by Fischer as being fraught with far greater problems of definition than that of the traditional biographer of an individual historical personality. Nevertheless, in reducing the alternatives to either a biographical-psychological historiography or one which seeks to explore the historical structures and tendencies, Fischer prefers the latter because it is able to range beyond the temporal and casual limitations imposed on the individual. But in opting for the second alternative, the historian is confronted with yet another decision, namely whether or not his object of enquiry is the state and its political life or the broader stream of supra-national cultural life.

If one chooses the state, one is concerned either with its power struggles with other states or with the internal class struggle and social rivalries, but in both cases the state always remains the basic unit of enquiry. In the second case, the permanent achievements of individuals or epochs must be recorded with the aim of portraying the development of human culture in which achievements from different epochs and areas are compared. The choice between these alternatives will of course be determined by what the historian regards as the purpose of historiography. In Germany, this used to be (until the passing of Gerhard Ritter) the science of the rulers; historiography was to serve the statesman so that he could find models and inspirations for future state-craft. History written with this goal in mind was simply the hand-maid of the state and rested ultimately on the Machiavellian concept of *raison d'état*.

In contrast to this there was the style of historiography favoured in the West which had the function of instructing the citizen in democratic values or of preparing him for participation in the process of checking or controlling the power of the state. Fischer observes that this political-pedagogic tendency in Western historiography rests on the optimistic assumption that the political institutions of the state can be reformed and that the citizen can be educated to play a responsible role in society. This type of historiography was also concerned with identifying generally valid propositions for the conduct of international affairs and for the promotion of international conciliation.

In this way Fischer contrasts the former German and the

Western schools of history as aristocratic and democratic respectively; the one designed to serve the needs of the monarch or his statesmen, the other tending to improve the political behaviour of electors and their parliamentary representatives. However, in either case the historian stands in a tradition which makes him a partisan for his own state whatever its form. Both traditions clearly lent themselves to exaggerations which could no longer satisfy the criteria of scholarship. And here Fischer raises the question whether or not historiography may or must make value judgments. Both traditions did this but with the difference that the German tradition denied that it did so. On the other hand, Western historiography saw it as part of its function to do so. So, enquires Fischer, is historical writing always concerned with value recognition? If this were the case, then the judgment of the historian of a situation, a process or a personality must always be made according to the yardsticks of that particular time. The German historicist tradition took this view, one which could lead to a complete relativising of values. On the other hand, the Western tradition which was orientated towards the Enlightenment tended to judge every phenomenon, every human action or culture — at least within the European context — with transcendental norms (*überhistorische Masstäbe*).

Fischer observes that modern international law since Grotius with its attempts to realise by means of international or supranational organisations has had very little success in controlling relations between states, though certain principles have been recognised as generally binding. However, experience had shown that whenever states have perceived their vital interests or honour threatened — factors which they themselves defined — they have sought to defend them without reference to international law. And further, even when war, as a means of policy, is embarked upon as a crusade or as a world police action to maintain some high principle, it can never be contemplated without reference to the facts of national *power*, the extension of *power* or the securing of *power* (emphasis provided). On the other hand, the natural law tradition and the values derived from it have in the domestic policies of states struck deeper roots, for example in the control of power by constitutional means and by the separation of powers.

This process is seen by Fischer actually to have developed in German states from the Age of Absolutism through to the concept of constitutional monarchy and finally to parliamentary democracy. Unfortunately, the latter development had been violently interrupted by the experience of the Third Reich but, paradoxically, now because of that experience the parliamentary form of government is all the more firmly established, and with it the historical-political ideas and values which originated in the Anglo-Saxon state tradition. This development has brought with it a concentration of historical interest on those processes which have either generated or retarded the growth of liberal and democratic concepts and institutions. And here Fischer has focused sharply on a critical political-pedagogic function of the historian. In carrying out his task of illuminating the historical process which produced the current form of the state in which he lives, the historian runs the risk of becoming a mere advocate of the state or indeed its propagandist. This is what happened in totalitarian states: the historian worked merely as a herald for the prevailing ideology and might not exercise any critical function. And Fischer warns his colleagues in West Germany that it is insufficient to be merely anti-communist since this would make one blind not only to the realities of power and changes within West Germany, but also to the developments which take place within the Communist and Third World — and not least in the West itself where there were crisis points of domestic tension.

So, the task of the historian, according to Fischer was to exercise a critical vigilance over trends within his own as well as other countries. The experience of the Third Reich has obviously convinced Fischer that the historicist tradition from Hegel and Ranke with its idealisation of the state and repudiation of value judgments had assigned to conservative German historians the role of court historians. They had been content to describe the evolution of the German nation and functioned as heralds of national policy. This had made them blind to the broader developments in the outside world, and when the Hitler tyranny was established, these national historians had been largely helpless to offer any meaningful criticism. Their long training in national introspection turned them into meek fellow travellers or at best inwardly disturbed onlookers of a civilization-destroying movement. This experience illustrated to them the untenability of their previous position and so, after 1945, when the new situation demanded the re-writing of German history for the current generation, Fischer was among the first to reflect on those elements in the historical-political tradition which had made National Socialism possible.

As Fischer has noted, the Anglo-Saxon historiographical tradition had taught people the rights and duties of the citizen with regard to the state, and it educated them to participate in political decision-making. This was because it drew inspiration from the Enlightenment tradition which assigned to historiography the task of applying humanistic norms to the historical process. While Fischer clearly recognises the problematic nature of the concept of transcendental norms, he is now convinced that in spite of the naivete which often characterises Anglo-Saxon writing about national and international politics, it is nevertheless dangerous to assume, in the Hegelian sense, that the state is a supra-personal agency with a divine mission that stands above the sphere of every-day morality, to which moral norms do not apply. That this kind of thinking contributed to the gross absurdities of the Third Reich can scarcely be denied. In order to illustrate "the corrupting influence of power", Fischer has focused on the power structure of the Wilhelmine Reich because he sees, as Ludwig Dehio saw earlier, that the "spirit and structure" of Prusso-German imperialism which had not disappeared after 1919 had made Hitler's success possible.[21] That is why Fischer determined to analyse the spirit and structure of Prusso-German imperialism in *War of Illusions*.

This outline of Fritz Fischer's historiographical position ought

[21] c.f. Ludwig Dehio, *Germany and World Politics in the Twentieth Century*, pp. 11–37.

to make clear what has motivated his scholarship. It also ought to explain how it is possible for a dissenter still to be a patriot. Fischer's historiographical aim is directed at cementing democratic values among his countrymen by pointing to the catastrophic results of earlier anti-democratic values. In his work the Wilhelmine Reich is revealed as a state racked with unresolved inner tensions. The leadership, being encapsulated in an anachronistic world view, were incapable of discovering the solutions because these would have had to be introduced from outside the prevailing Prusso-German constitutional concepts. Under these conditions evolutionary social change was quite impossible. The Bismarckian-Wilhelmine Empire had through the intellectual-historical tradition of its founding manoeuvred itself into a corner from which it could not retreat. The basic structural difficulty was the Bismarckian constitution and the social-ideological assumptions upon which it rested.

Subsequent research (whether stimulated directly by Fischer or by others) has served to reinforce Fischer's conclusions about the nature of the Bismarckian-Wilhelmine power structure.[22] Although there are critics who accuse Fischer of "onesidedness", they have had to admit that the discussion stimulated by his work has led to a methodological "revision" in German historiography in which the social-historical and structural factors that Fischer has described are more and more in evidence.[23]

What has shocked Fischer's critics most about *War of Illusions* is the compelling case he has built up to show that the nation was not only "ideologically prepared" for a war of expansion, but that also by 1912 the idea of a war to solve both domestic and foreign policy difficulties was dominating the

[22] These historians, whose relevant works are listed in the bibliography, and who have either been pupils of Fischer or identify with his approach, include the following: Berghahn, Böhme, Geiss, Guratzsch, Kaelbele, Puhle, Stegmann, Sywottek, Vogel, vom Brocke, Wehler, Wernecke and Witt.

[23] Hans Mommsen, "Haupttendenzen nach 1945 und in der Ära des kalten Krieges", in *Geschichtswissenschaft in Deutschland*, ed. Bernd Faulenbach, p. 120.

mind of the power-elite. In a real sense *War of Illusions* is built around the fact that the Kaiser held a so-called "War Council" with service chiefs on 8 December 1912. The discussion concerning this will be dealt with in the next chapter.

CHAPTER II

From War Council to War

Whoever closes his eyes to the long range significance
[of the war council] has apparently still not compre-
hended the decisive element in the late Wilhelmine
empire: its nature as a military state.

ADOLF GASSER,
*Der deutsche Hegemonialkrieg
von 1914*, p. 312

Most critics of Fritz Fischer now accept his view that Germany
deliberately unleashed the First World War. What they still
strongly dispute is that it was calculated for long in advance.
They prefer to regard the German decision to start a preventive
war against Russia and France by urging Austria to attack
Serbia in July–August 1914 as being one forced upon her by
circumstances which made it necessary for the Reich to seize
the initiative in order to preserve national sovereignty and that
of the ally, Austria–Hungary. For this reason, Fischer's assertion in *War of Illusions* that at the latest the war was calculated
for in December 1912 has stirred up the critics once again. They
are not convinced that the now notorious war council of 8
December 1912 had any real bearing on what happened in
July–August 1914. On that date at the end of 1912 the Kaiser
had summoned a meeting of service chiefs (the Army Chief of
Staff, von Moltke and the three admirals, von Tirpitz, von
Müller and von Heeringen). The Chancellor, Bethmann-
Hollweg, was not present.

The occasion for the meeting was Wilhelm II's intense anger
at the British reaction to a quite bellicose speech in the Reichstag
on 2 December 1912 by the German Chancellor. The latter had

pledged German military aid to Austria, "if Austria in the course of securing her vital interests . . . is attacked by Russia". The British war minister Lord Haldane, acting in collusion with his foreign secretary, Sir Edward Grey, had responded with an unequivocal statement via the German ambassador in London, Prince Lichnowsky, making the point that Britain could not tolerate a shift in the balance of power in Europe which might result from an Austrian invasion of Serbia. Since Germany had expected Britain to remain neutral in a conflict emerging in Eastern Europe, the Kaiser was understandably put out. His reason for convening the meeting of service chiefs was to take an inventory of Germany's capacity to wage war against the Entente. The outcome of their deliberations was that the army represented by von Moltke desired a military showdown aimed at destroying Russia's growth in power as soon as possible — "the sooner the better". The navy represented by von Tirpitz was not so anxious to get started because the ship and canal building programme then under way would take another year to complete.[1]

The questions raised here for the historian are very important for the correct assessment of Imperial Germany's intentions up to July–August 1914. In the light of the most recent research, is it possible to look upon the "war council" as nothing more than a snap, angry reaction of the mercurial Kaiser to a sudden irritation from Britain, with absolutely no political consequence whatever? In other words, should the whole affair be dismissed by scholars because the Kaiser was well known to be an emotional and temperamental person whose fits of pique as well as his pathetic attempts to play the Supreme War Lord were not to be taken seriously by any responsible officials? This, of course, could be true. On the other hand it could equally be true that this time the Kaiser was *not* play-acting and that the statements by the service chiefs were not made simply to humour their theatrical monarch. What is to be made of this? A few serious historians state unreservedly that it is absurd to

[1] J. C. G. Röhl, "V. Admiral von Müller and the Approach of the War, 1911–1914", *HJ* XII (1969), pp. 659–662.

attribute any importance whatever to the "war council of 8 December 1912".[2]

The only way to gain some clarity on this issue is to examine the strongest arguments for and against the significance of the "war council" because such argumentation is the very essence of historiography. Historical information, as E. H. Carr has pointed out, only becomes historical fact if the historians choose to make it so.[3] For some the "war council" is a fact of profound historical significance, while for others it only clouds our understanding of the real issues.

Precise knowledge about the "war council" was discovered for the first time by Dr. J. C. G. Röhl of the University of Sussex although, as he himself notes, Professor W. Hubatsch of Bonn, one of Fischer's most rabid opponents, had seen the relevant documents and actually quoted from them in 1958. He did not, however, recognise their significance.[4] The documents in question were the diaries of Admiral Georg Alexander von Müller, Chief of the Kaiser's Naval Cabinet from 1906 to 1918. His papers are now located in the *Bundesarchiv* in Coblenz. A version of these had been published by Walter Görlitz in 1965 but this material had previously been carefully edited by the admiral and it omits the critical reference to the "war council" of 8 December 1912.[5] In checking the published version against the original manuscript, Röhl has been able to fill in certain gaps in our knowledge of the course of German policy in the years prior to the outbreak of war in 1914.

For Röhl some of these gaps are of vital significance, for he believes that the new data indicate very clearly that in the three years prior to the outbreak of war, "the German leaders were less concerned with the question of whether to begin a war than

---

[2] See for example Wolfgang J. Mommsen, "Die deutsche 'Weltpolitik' und der erste Weltkrieg", *NPL* XVI (1971), Andreas Hillgruber, *Deutschlands Rolle in der Vorgeschichte der beiden Weltkriege,* and L. C. F. Turner's review of J. C. G. Röhl, *Delusion or Design* in *AJPH* XX (1974), pp. 121–124.

[3] E. H. Carr, *What is History?*, p. 12.

[4] Röhl, "V. Admiral von Müller ≠ ≠ ≠ ", p. 652.

[5] Ibid., fn. 9.

with the question of how and when a war might best be begun".[6]
This conclusion seems eminently reasonable when a survey of
the thrust of German policy in those years is made. The framework of this policy was outlined by Bethmann Hollweg when he
assumed office in July 1909. It contained the following seven
goals:

(1) Neutrality pact with Britain in the event of being
    attacked by Russia and France together or separately;
    also in the event of Russia attacking Austria-Hungary,
    a fact which would require German assistance to the
    latter.

(2) A means of gaining this promise of neutrality from
    Britain would be a naval agreement but that would only
    be of use to Germany if it simultaneously was linked
    to a peaceful policy by Britain towards Germany.

(3) In this respect only those concessions could be made in
    naval policy which did not affect the current naval policy
    of the Reich.

(4) Such a naval policy would then pave the way for a poli-
    tical agreement with Britain which would enhance
    Germany's position within the European concert
    decisively.

(5) Such a strengthening of Germany's political status would
    improve the Chancellor's position with regard to extre-
    mists who regarded a conciliatory naval policy towards
    Britain as a sign of weakness.

(6) This policy should be conducted as far as possible inde-
    pendently of the *Reichstag* and should not be sacrificed
    to other agreements such as the Baghdad railway, colo-
    nial questions or a commercial treaty which would have
    to be initiated if Britain went over to a protective tariff.

(7) The negotiations must be so conducted that in the event
    of their breaking down, the blame will be laid at Britain's
    door.[7]

[6] Ibid., p. 673.   [7] Fischer, *Krieg* . . . , pp. 109–110.

It is important to note that this policy had the approval of both Admiral von Tirpitz and the Kaiser and that it formed the basis of Bethmann's negotiations with the British ambassador from mid-October 1909 onwards. This policy, however, in requiring a promise of British neutrality, was doomed to failure; it bound Britain too far in advance and would have led to a change in the balance of power tantamount to a German hegemony on the Continent. In this respect, Bethmann's policy was based on an illusion, namely that Britain would look on indifferently while Germany annihilated France again as in 1870–71.[8]

Because these Anglo-German neutrality talks proved fruitless, Germany once again turned her attention to Russia with whom a minor agreement over the Baghdad railway was achieved, the purpose being to demonstrate a German-Russian rapprochement. But even here the veiled intention had been to detach Russia from Britain so that the latter would be more ready to turn to Germany. And it appeared that this move had had the desired effect since Britain did indeed begin to make overtures to Germany in 1910.[9]

However, as Bethmann Hollweg explained to the *Reichstag* on 2nd December 1914, the British had only been prepared to negotiate on questions which were of peripheral importance to the Germans; at no time would the British abandon the basic constant of their foreign policy and stand by to allow one Continental power to erect an hegemony over the others. However, it had been Bethmann's aim, by virtue of growing German power, both naval and political, to show that the old British principle was no longer tenable. In other words, German strength would become so great that it would constitute a risk for Britain to stand in her way. Germany was, in short, being held in check by Britain [10] — a fact which the Reich leadership felt to be becoming more and more intolerable. Indeed, from 1911 until 1914 Germany conducted her foreign policy with the precise aim of overcoming the traditional British control of the balance of power. The basic device in pursuing this policy was

[8] Ibid., p. 112.   [9] Ibid., p. 113.   [10] Ibid., p. 115.

to indicate to the other Powers that Germany was at all times prepared to force issues to the extreme in order to gain her will — the device of the calculated risk.

Also, from 1910 onwards it was clear that only an aggressive foreign policy would overcome the fragmentation of the political parties in the *Reichstag*. In that year the Social Democrats recovered dramatically in by-elections from their losses in the 1907 general elections. And in order successfully to check an upsurge of socialist political influence the government would have to attempt to unite all the anti-socialist parties by pursuing a vigorous and daring foreign policy — "a mobilisation of national instincts".[11]

With this background the course of German diplomacy in the "Agadir crisis" of 1911 becomes clear. Morocco was a golden opportunity for Germany to force France into conceding some of that North African territory for its iron ore resources. Also, the Foreign Secretary, Kiderlen-Wächter, was impatient for a success prior to the *Reichstag* elections due in 1912.[12] The entire business shows to what extent the German leadership was anxious to force the pace in order to secure what was left of the earth's surface — "it is the last opportunity, without fighting, to acquire something useful in Africa",[13] and was to be the means of "bluffing" a neighbouring power. However, Britain was aware what a diplomatic reverse for France would do to the *Entente Cordiale,* particularly as Russia at that time did not make any special signs of supporting France.

It was recognised correctly in Britain that Germany was playing for the highest possible stakes — a diplomatic defeat of France would result in a virtual breaking up of the *Entente* and so the support of France in this second Morocco crisis was seen in London as absolutely vital.[14] In her view, Britain had no choice but to stand by France — an attitude which was made perfectly clear to Germany by Lloyd George in his famous Mansion House speech. German enthusiasm for the annexation of Morocco had, of course, been raised to boiling point, and so,

[11] Ibid., p. 117. [12] Ibid., p. 118.
[13] Ibid., p. 123. [14] Ibid., p. 126.

when German diplomacy failed to bluff France into handing over Morocco, and had to be content with virtually worthless compensations in French Congo, the public reaction in Germany was one of white fury. The outcome of this crisis which had been provoked by Germany was regarded as a humiliating rebuff to national prestige and the blame was placed squarely on Britain's doorstep — the Power which had blocked Germany's justifiable expansionist ambitions.[15]

Seldom had a Power taken such a diplomatic defeat so tragically — it was regarded as a national humiliation comparable to Olmütz, Prussia's humiliation when Austria forced her to give up plans for uniting Germany in 1850; the press attacked the Chancellor, and the Colonial Secretary, Lindequist, resigned in protest. Of course, the attacks on Bethmann had bordered on the hysterical but he was aware that to press any harder would have resulted in war against an unfavourable coalition. "It is my duty to conduct affairs in such a way that a war which can be avoided and is not required by German honour is avoided."[16]

Bethmann therefore tried to interpret the outcome of the Morocco crisis in the best possible light and was genuinely disturbed that the German people had so frivolously ventured to the brink of war.[17] He was further angered by the acrimony of the anti-British outbursts from responsible quarters and was more concerned with coming to some understanding with Britain than a favourable election result brought about by embarrassingly chauvinistic anti-British hysteria.[18]

The election year 1912 saw above all a revival of the Social Democrats who polled 110 seats which caused the government serious concern about their real ability to get "vital" legislation through the *Reichstag*,[19] especially if the Progressives formed a block (on some issues) with the Socialists. This depressing prospect caused an upsurge of both anti-democratic and anti-semitic propaganda in so-called "national quarters", i.e. Pan-German, industrialist and agricultural. Under these circum-

---

[15] Ibid., pp. 137–144.   [16] Ibid., p. 139.
[17] Ibid., p. 142.   [18] Ibid., p. 143.   [19] Ibid., p. 149.

stances the Chancellor felt it his duty to spell out his so-called
"policy of diagonals". He asserted that the Reich would be
governed neither democratically nor in a reactionary style. The
task of the future lay not in the direction of a further democratisation but rather in the extension of national power. Above
all there must be unity in order to achieve that aim. "History
will mercilessly tread underfoot that state which cripples its
efficiency through discord."[20] And the degree of discord in the
Reichstag was evident in the election results — a fact which
gained eloquent expression in the debacle over the election of
a new speaker (*Reichstagspräsident*).[21] The entire result of the
1912 election indicated, in short, how really ineffectual a foreign
policy designed to "mobilise national instincts" in fact was. On
the contrary, a polarisation process was in evidence; as the SPD
increased the number of its mandates, so on the other hand the
representatives of industry and agriculture drew closer together.
The common hostility to the SPD in the past did not, of course,
imply a community of aims on other issues. However, the feeling in "national quarters" against the Social Democrats had by
1912 reached a degree of bitterness which was only matched by
the ignorance prevailing about them. It was not widely appreciated in fact that influential revisionists in the SPD were not
opposed to naval and military expenditure in principle.[22]

However, certain patriots were so concerned with Germany's
foreign policy reverses as well as the depressing result of the
general elections that it was deemed necessary to found an army
league to make propaganda for an increased military establishment.[23] This so-called *Wehrverein* was officially a non-party
organisation like the Pan-German League which energetically
supported its aims. It was nothing more than an unadorned
war-mongering, imperialistic pressure group which managed to
unite under its slogans all parties with the exception of the
SPD and the left-wing liberals.[24] The *Wehrverein* was extra-
ordinarily successful in its pressure group activity. The
Rheinisch-Westfälische Zeitung of 12 March 1913 commented,

[20] Ibid., p. 157.   [21] Ibid., p. 165.
[22] Ibid., p. 159.   [23] Ibid.   [24] Ibid., p. 162.

"The government has adopted all the demands which the *Wehrverein* in cooperation with the General Staff has been championing most energetically in public over the last months . . . In short everything . . . which the *Wehrverein* has been demanding . . . is now to be fulfilled."[25]

The importance of this activity lies in the fact that despite the apparent landslide to the left in the *Reichstag*, the imperialistic foreign policy and "security measures" of the German government could be carried out with relative ease. It was only in domestic politics that intra-party friction became obvious,[26] and again, this parliamentary discord enabled the Chancellor to rule without fear of the *Reichstag;* no consolidated blocks could be formed to oppose government policy.

This self-emasculation of the *Reichstag* was to prove disastrous for Germany. Only the 110 Social Democrats constituted any kind of consistent opposition but even they were becoming increasingly quiescent and conciliatory when one considers their official "revolutionary" aims. Nevertheless, their general opposition to imperialism was highly suspect; the Centre Party leader, Erzberger, expressed this attitude in May 1914, when he said that in the age of national expansion of the Reich, 110 Social Democrats constituted a ball and chain for the entire policy and he believed that, as before, the destruction of the "mighty power" of social democracy was the greatest problem posed for the domestic politics of the Reich.[27] Of course, this attitude was based on a misunderstanding of the true character of the SPD because the Socialists proved in the event to be as patriotic as the other parties of the *Reichstag*. Nevertheless, their existence served to make the originally more moderate parties extremely chauvinistic in foreign policy issues. It is against this background (which shows the "primacy of domestic policy") that German foreign policy must be evaluated.

The Balkan war, which had broken out on 8 October 1912, became a critical test for German policy. The foreign secretary, Kiderlen-Waechter, as Röhl notes, was concerned to maintain European peace by restraining Austria who was anxious to

[25] Ibid., p. 163.   [26] Ibid., p. 164.   [27] Ibid., p. 168.

prevent Serbia gaining a port on the Adriatic.[28] However, his attitude aroused considerable suspicions in Vienna that Germany was not solidly behind Austria-Hungary. In order to counter this impression, the Chancellor, Bethmann Hollweg, wished to be free to declare German support for Austria, should she become involved in a war with Serbia over the latter's attempt to secure an Adriatic port.[29] This was the background to the Chancellor's speech in the *Reichstag* on 2 December 1912 when he pledged German support, "if Austria in the course of securing her vital interests . . . is attacked by Russia".[30]

The significance of this calculation lay in the German belief that Britain would not concern herself over this issue. At the time authorities in Berlin thought they had reason to hope that relations with London were actually improving. Indeed, now as previously, good relations with Britain were of paramount importance in the German foreign policy conception. That is why the Kaiser reacted with such vehemence to Lord Haldane's warning that Britain "would find it impossible to remain neutral in a continental war resulting from an Austrian invasion of Serbia. Britain was committed to upholding the balance of power in Europe and could consequently not tolerate the crushing of France by Germany's superior military strength."[31]

Immediately on receiving Lichnowsky's report of his conversation with Haldane, the Kaiser summoned the service chiefs.[32] Admiral von Müller recorded the details in his diary. What Röhl regards as possibly a most significant indication of the continuity of German policy between December 1912 and August 1914 was the Kaiser's understanding of the power constellation: "The Kaiser opened the conference by envisaging the exact sequence of events of July 1914: Austria would attack Serbia, Russia would intervene on Serbia's behalf, and Germany would find herself at war with Russia, France and Great Britain."[33]

Fischer in his detailed analysis of subsequent policy has built upon Röhl's findings. Bethmann Hollweg had been sought out

---

[28] Röhl, "V. Admiral von Müller . . . ", p. 659.   [29] Ibid.
[30] Ibid., p. 660.   [31] Ibid.   [32] Ibid., p. 661.   [33] Ibid., p. 672.

on the same afternoon as the "war council" by von Müller who had stressed to him the necessity of preparing the nation via the press for a war arising out of an Austro-Serbian conflict. As Fischer notes, it is not possible to establish with certainty how the Chancellor was informed of the desire of both the Kaiser and von Moltke for a war to take place. However, within a week of the "war council" he himself was pressing the Kaiser for the necessary preparations for a large-scale war. He wanted, however, to maintain personal control of the press propaganda since he apparently had reservations about letting the army and navy ministries take charge of that.[34]

Before leaving the issue of the actual "war council" at which the Chancellor was not present, it is necessary to stress three things. First, the other German governments (i.e. of the federated states) had been notified via their military attachés in Berlin. The reports of the Bavarian and Saxon officials are extant. They apparently regarded the meeting with the utmost gravity.[35] The fact that decisions were taken by the Kaiser and the service chiefs on the desirability of war without consulting the head of the national government does not seem to have much concerned the federal states. Nor could it have especially offended Bethmann himself who seems to have accepted the decisions without demurring.

The second point concerns an entry by von Müller in his diary about the outcome of the "war council". Having noted that von Moltke had wanted war, and "the sooner the better", von Müller observed that the army chief had not drawn the correct conclusions, namely the need to confront both Russia and France with an ultimatum which would unleash a war with *the right on the German side*.[36] Since von Moltke had not suggested the means by which logical diplomatic follow-up could have been made after the "war council", von Müller wrote that the total result of their deliberations was virtually nil (*Das Ergebnis war so ziemlich null*).[37] In von Müller's view, then, the "war council" led to no concrete results, particularly

---

[34] Fischer, *Krieg* . . . , pp. 235–236.
[35] Ibid., pp. 234–235.
[36] Ibid. (emphasis added).
[37] Ibid., p. 234.

in view of the fact that von Tirpitz had opposed the idea of war until the naval and canal building programme was more advanced. Nevertheless, it would be quite unrealistic for historians to ignore the "war council", even though it indicated that the German leaders appreciated that Britain would now not remain neutral in a war involving France.

The third point emerges from this observation. Did the German government in fact from December 1912 onwards regard Britain as an implacable foe whose enmity would cancel out any German plans to change the balance of power on the Continent? Fischer shows that Bethmann Hollweg did not assess the British warning as seriously as the Kaiser apparently did.[38] The Chancellor simply took it to be an expression of Britain's determination not to allow Germany to annihilate France. So long as one could convince the British that Germany had no intention of this one could continue to reckon on British neutrality. In other words, the British warning was not taken by Bethmann to be grounds for abandoning the basis of his foreign policy conception. He still believed as before that continuing cooperation with Britain on individual issues would guarantee British neutrality in the coming conflict.

Fischer is very solidly supported in these conclusions by the Swiss historian, Adolf Gasser, who argues strongly for the view that the "war council" was the sure signal for a German intention to unleash a war as soon as certain preconditions were fulfilled. He maintains that anyone who will not see that the decisions of the "war council" were in fact carried out has still failed to comprehend the essential character of late Wilhelmine Germany, namely "its nature as a military state".[39] By this he means that in contrast to other "civilized" states the military in Wilhelmine Germany were the real decision-making element — not the "civilian leaders". In Professor Gasser's analysis of the "war council" he sees the war as being made conditional on the fulfilment of three conditions. The first was that the navy be sufficiently strong and concentrated to meet

[38] Ibid., pp. 237–238.
[39] Adolf Gasser, "Der deutsche Hegemonialkrieg von 1914", p. 312.

the possibility of British intervention. Actually, the General Staff was not as concerned about this as the Kaiser and von Tirpitz. The latter wanted to *postpone* the great struggle for eighteen months, until after the Kiel canal had been widened to allow Dreadnought-class battleships to pass through and the Heligoland harbour had been prepared for U-boats. Although the General Staff was not overly concerned with naval preparations, believing correctly in the event that the final decision in a contest of arms would be made on land, they had to give in to von Tirpitz's demands for a postponement of the war. This was because any premature challenge to Britain would have placed the very existence of the German navy in jeopardy.[40] It was vital to have the Kiel canal navigable for the largest battleships. This would have been of enormous significance in a war against both Britain and Russia. Otherwise the danger of piecemeal destruction of the German navy would have been very great.

A further reason for giving in to the navy on this point was that if the canal was fully usable, the navy could virtually guarantee to hinder any landing attempts, either by the British or the Russians on the North Sea or Baltic coasts. Indeed, as Gasser points out, the ultimate success of the Schlieffen plan rested on the army's ability to concentrate most of its forces in the west. The need to divert troops to ward off any landings would have weakened the chances of success from the beginning. For this reason the army could have no logical objection to the navy's demands to delay any hostilities. Professor Gasser asserts emphatically that it was these compelling reasons which forced von Moltke as well as the Kaiser to wait before unleashing a war. By the summer of 1914, however, the necessary extensions on the Kiel canal had been completed and on 23 June 1914 with the passage through it of the *Hohenzollern* it was officially opened — although the depth was still insufficient to allow a ship of the line through fully laden. Nevertheless, there were no more obstacles to getting any battleship from one sea to the other with "empty bunkers". Bunkering could be accomplished

[40] Ibid., p. 316.

on either side. As Gasser notes, therewith the most important obstacle to unleashing a "three-front war" was removed, four days before the assassination at Sarajevo.[41]

The second pre-condition for a *Blitzkrieg* according to Gasser, was the successful passing of a new army bill. The sources available on the war council indicate that the Kaiser instructed the war minister on the next day to prepare a "large army bill" — *eine grosse Heeresvorlage*.[42] Von Moltke had already begun working for this in November. The Chancellor, too, lent his immediate support. On 8 January 1913 there began to appear the first commentaries in the press about the projected army increases. On 1 March the government proposal to meet the enormous cost involved was made known. It proposed an *ad hoc* property tax which precipitated an acrimonious debate in the *Reichstag*. Finally, the bill was approved on 30 June 1913.[43]

At the same time the German General Staff (which Gasser sees as the supreme authority in the Reich) began to institute the necessary strategic measures to ensure the success of a lightning war. In this connection the Schlieffen plan was modified to enable a German attack on the Belgian city of Liége immediately after the mobilisation order. As Gasser observes, this was a change of the greatest political consequence — a rigidly established plan to attack Belgium whose neutrality was guaranteed by all Great Powers — including Britain. The small state of Belgium was not to be allowed any time to place its most important centre of defence on a war footing. With this plan, von Moltke deprived his government of any possibility during the 8 to 10 day German mobilisation period of a last-minute chance of preserving peace because of the military necessity of occupying Liége before the Belgians could reinforce it. But, as Gasser notes, the fact that this military decision automatically restricted the government's manouvreability meant

---

[41] Ibid., p. 317.

[42] Ibid., p. 318.

[43] For a detailed discussion of the political in-fighting over this army bill, particularly how to fianance it, see Fischer, *Krieg* . . . , pp. 251–269, and also Dieter Groh, *Negative Integration* ، . . , pp. 423–452.

absolutely nothing to the generals who had already in any case determined in principle at the end of 1912 to unleash a war.

The critical point which Gasser also raises here is that neither Kaiser nor Chancellor were instructed concerning the planned surprise attack on Liége. The Chief of Staff, von Moltke, had done this as if he were responsible to no one but Almighty God. In the summer of 1915 he said, justifying himself, "With this operation I put everything on one card and won the gamble thanks to the bravery of our troops".[44] Indeed, the initial phase of the modified Schlieffen was a success but the overall operation a disaster.[45] Germany's "militarised foreign policy"[46] reaped its reward in Versailles. It is this fact which Gasser is at pains to stress: The German Empire founded by Bismarck in 1871 had become at the latest by 1912 thoroughly dominated by the army. The generals' perspective on policy excluded all other considerations. Having established this, Gasser introduces the third precondition for the unleashing of the war. This was the question of winning the support of all sections of the German population for a war against Russia.

To this end, both the navy and the army general staff were concerned to exploit the German press at least from the time of the "war council". In addition, German policy towards Russia was designed to provoke her, and in this Bethmann

[44] Quoted after Adolf Gasser, "Deutschlands Entschluss zum Präventivkrieg 1913/14", p. 190, fn. 71.

[45] Gasser, "Der deutsche Hegemonialkrieg . . . ", p. 319.

[46] c.f. Jehuda L. Wallach, *Das Dogma der Vernichtungsschlacht*, p. 108, where the author comments that in Schlieffen's plan the question of the political consequences was never considered. This is further elaborated on pp. 296–303 where the German generals in the period 1890 to 1914 are shown to have exercised a dominating influence not only on war aims but also, by virtue of imposing a rigid war plan on the "civilian" statesmen, on foreign policy. German foreign policy was conducted on the firm premiss of a two-front war, i.e. simultaneously with Russia and France. This was virtually a permanent assumption since Schlieffen had become Chief-of-Staff in 1891. For this reason, the German government never developed a flexible war plan. All they had was Schlieffen's directives for a two-front campaign, nothing else. The disastrous consequences for German foreign policy only became evident in the July-August crisis 1914. See Wallach's discussion on pp. 62–63.

Hollweg fully concurred with the generals' conception. As Gasser notes, German foreign policy was conducted according to the directives of the general staff until the summer of 1914. It had the task of intensifying the provocation of Russia and of holding Austria-Hungary back from any precipitate action against Serbia which would have unleashed a war prematurely.[47] All this functioned supremely well. The idea of an unavoidable final struggle between the Germanic and Slavic races was becoming established in the Reich. The Russians were provoked by the appointment of the German general, Liman von Sanders, to take command of Turkish troops in the Constantinople-Bosphorus region. This was the most sensitive area for Russian security as well as commerce.

Coupled with the concomitant anti-Russian press campaign these measures succeeded in provoking Russian nationalism to such an extent that Petersburg responded in April 1914 with an increase in the customs duties on grain from Germany. These came into force on 12 June 1914 and had the desired effect of alienating the one particularly pro-Russian group within the Reich, the East Elbian Junkers.[48] Therewith, the three pre-conditions for a war were fulfilled, a war which the German generals wished to start on terms as favourable to the Reich as possible. As Gasser sums it up, the Kiel Canal was ready, the army prepared for its lightning attack in the west, and the nation united from the Junkers to the proletariat in a virtually uniform Russophobia.[49]

All that remained was to find or invent a suitable pretext on which to prod Austria into action. There were any number of flash points in the Balkans which would supply Austria with the

[47] Gasser, "Der deutsche Hegemonialkrieg", pp. 320–322. In trying to stir up anti-Russian sentiment Bethmann addressed the *Reichstag* on 7 April 1913 on the danger of a European conflagration which would see the Germanic races locked in combat with the Slavic. Gasser maintains that it is untenable to regard this speech of the Chancellor as a "slip", as Wolfgang J. Mommsen ("Die deutsche 'Weltpolitik' . . . ", p. 490) attempts. Rather it was a calculated provocation.
[48] Ibid., p. 322.
[49] Ibid., p. 323.

necessary excuse to intervene with the resultant challenge to Russia. However, when the murder of the Crown Prince occurred it was welcomed in Berlin as the beckoning of fate which, as von Moltke is reported to have said, provided an unusually favourable opportunity to strike which ought to be exploited.[50] This indeed occurred. The Dual Alliance between Berlin and Vienna for defensive purposes was transformed into an offensive alliance, and the hesitant Austria urged beyond her intentions to act against Serbia. This is indicated by Berlin's pressure on Vienna concerning the nature of the ultimatum to Belgrade. As both Fischer and Gasser emphasise, there was no danger of attack on the Reich or Austria-Hungary from Russia. The German government intentionally tried to awaken the impression among all subjects that the nation had to defend itself. In this it was totally successful. As Admiral von Müller remarked on 1 August 1914: "The mood is brilliant. The government has succeeded very well in making us appear as the attacked."[51]

The information provided by Röhl about the "war council" of 8 December 1912 and the interpretation of it by Gasser show it to be a "historical fact" of some profound significance. However, as already indicated, there are those who, unlike Professor Fischer, try to suggest that it is bad history to take any notice of the "war council". To this, one can only reply that many an historical monograph has been written on much flimsier evidence than Röhl, Fischer or Gasser have adduced and have never been subjected to the same virulent criticism. It is really because the critics are politically embarrassed by these findings that they carp so importunately. They are reluctant to accept the image of Imperial Germany and of their national heroes which the revisionists have projected. Such a critic is Wolfgang J. Mommsen. He does accredit Fischer with having clarified aspects of German history in this period and remarks that although Fischer's theses had been emotionally rejected at first,

[50] Ibid.
[51] Röhl, "V. Admiral von Müller . . ", p. 670.

they have since been accepted as valid.[52] However, Mommsen will not accept that the 1914 war and the German war aims were the product of decisions made in influential circles much earlier than July 1914. In other words, Mommsen denies Fischer's basic thesis that the German Reich since its foundation was striving continuously to reach world power status and that the First World War was a logical extension of this growing political will.

Mommsen enquires what Fischer means by "continuity", and believes he has destroyed Fischer's thesis by pointing out that individual leaders changed their mind on policy from time to time. For example, Mommsen accuses Fischer of asserting that during the Agadir crisis of 1911, the real "hawks" among the German leaders were Kiderlen-Wächter, the foreign secretary, and the generals while the Kaiser was a "dove" or a procrastinator. A year later at the peak of the Balkan crisis the Kaiser is reported as having reversed his position and is depicted as lusting for war. Without consulting his Chancellor he demanded that the nation be psychologically prepared for war. Further, Mommsen, who defends Bethmann Hollweg, refuses to accept that the Chancellor believed that Germany's domestic and foreign policy problems could be solved by a war as Fischer would have it. Indeed, Fischer depicted Bethmann as blowing hot and cold, and only identified an unalterable will to war on the part of the generals. And even this is doubted by Mommsen because it was by no means clear whether the generals wanted war or were merely acting as officers must, namely to plan as though war could eventuate at any time.

Because of this, Mommsen asks, who in fact in the Reich was (were) the decisive bearer(s) of the will to war for the conquest of world power? Was it the civilian government, the Kaiser, the service chiefs, the patriotic organisations, certain parties or the

[52] In numerous articles. He has been described by L. C. F. Turner as one of Fischer's ablest critics (see Turner's review article referred to in footnote no. 2). Mommsen's displeasure with Fischer's "second" book is expressed forcibly in his review article, "Die deutsche 'Weltpolitik' und der erste Weltkrieg", though he is not entirely negative. See his remarks on p. 483 of this article.

"nation" in its entirety?[53] All that could be said of Fischer's narrative was that the key actors kept changing their roles. Mommsen is clearly irritated by Fischer's alleged tendency to lump all together under the one common denominator of imperialism. If one looked more closely it would be seen that there were many variations in the goals of the distinct groups as well as differences in the degree of aggression. For this reason one could not speak of a uniform political will nor of a continuity of imperialistic goals. In Mommsen's view the First World War did not result from specifically German aims crystallised over a long period but rather was simply an *ad hoc* German reaction to a sudden crisis situation, whereby he concedes that the German leadership took the initiative to unleash a preventive war. With this conviction, Mommsen cannot attribute any special importance to the "war council" of 8 December 1912 which for Fischer was the turning point of German policy before 1914.[54] Mommsen's chief objection to this thesis is that the Chancellor was not only not a party to the war council (which was just a hysterical reaction of the Kaiser) but also afterwards disassociated himself from it and indeed actually warned the generals against colluding with the Kaiser without his knowledge and also against their stirring up the press to make propaganda for a war.[55]

These protests by Mommsen are merely despairing attempts to place the Chancellor in a more responsible light. If Bethmann warned the generals neither to go behind his back in future nor to intervene with the press, it means simply that he had to

[53] Ibid., p. 485.
[54] Ibid., p. 488.
[55] Ibid., p. 489. c.f. L. C. F. Turner's criticism of Röhl (footnote no. 2). The Australian professor tends to overlook the point being made repeatedly by the Fischer school that the German government was effectively "militarised" from 1911 onwards. It will not do simply to regard isolated admonitions to caution by individual statesmen or generals as "proofs" of Imperial Germany's essentially "harmless" foreign policy. Professor Turner in his desire to be scrupulously fair has paid undue attention to the subtle anti-Fischer criticisms of such patriotic German notables as Gerhard Ritter, Egmont Zechlin and Erwin Hölzle as well as Wolfgang J. Mommsen.

exert himself in peripheral matters so as to give the appearance
that the Chancellor's office was one of some consequence. In
reality it was a very weak office which Bethmann himself
recognised.[56] Such criticisms of Fischer's work as Mommsen
makes also fail to take into account that despite the variety of
imperialistic goals from the different pressure groups there are
undeniably "clusters of ideas" which they all had in common.[57]

[56] For a telling admission by Bethmann of the weakness of his
position see the statement he made to the French ambassador, Jules
Cambon, on the occasion of the Kaiser's birthday reception on 27
January 1914: "Je suis attaqué de tous les côtés et il est possible que je
ne reste pas longtemps à la tête des affairs, mais cela m'est indifférent",
(quoted from Fischer, *Krieg* . . . , p. 642).

[57] The term "clusters of ideas" was suggested to me by my colleague
Dr. J. Siracusa. It is taken from the work of Bernard Bailyn, *The
Ideological Origins of the American Revolution*, p. 33. Mommsen tries
to make too much of the point that there were varieties of emphasis
in the political will across the spectrum of imperialist publicists, entre-
preneurs and officials in the Reich. As Bailyn points out concerning
what the Germans would call the "formation of political will" prior to
the American Revolution, the writings of the politically aware "reveal
not merely positions taken but the reasons why positions were taken;
they reveal motive and understanding: the assumptions, beliefs and
ideas—the articulated world-view that lay behind the manifest events
of the time" (p. vi). Just as there was a range of propositions which
united the American colonists against the various characteristics perceived by them to be oppressive, the German "patriots" of the
Wilhelmine era united under a common denominator, namely the all-
pervading belief in the rightness of the German mission in the world.
Certainly, the "manifest events of the time" in July-August 1914 up until
November 1918 had very few influential critics in Germany. In other
words, in those circles which considered themselves truly "national" the
idea of the German mission continued in general to be propagated.
One of the most striking vindications of Fischer's position is the
patriotic "mobilisation of the intellectuals" in Germany at the outbreak
of war. (See Klaus Schwabe, *Wissenschaft und Kriegsmoral*). The point
is that if, as Mommsen maintains, there were really moderate spirits in
Germany, one would have expected to find them among university
professors actively criticising national policy. There were, of course,
very few. Instead, there was a widespread endorsement of the German
mission which would indicate the strength of the German imperialistic
ideology in the pre-war period. See the present writer's "Pan Germanism
and the German Professors".

It is now well known that Bethmann's reservations were not those of a humanitarian or liberal statesman, but rather induced by a fear that if the politically insensitive military had their way entirely they would bungle things by being too openly over-zealous for war and arouse undesirable suspicions both within and outside the country of the Reich's intentions.[58] As Fischer has forcefully stated, "there is not a single document in the world which could weaken the central truth, that in July 1914 a will to war existed solely and alone on the German side and that all arrangements on the side of the *Entente* served the defensive security of their alliance."[59] And that will to war had been crystallising for many years previously.

[58] Bethmann's lack of confidence in the senior military personnel of his country to behave with the tact and subtlety necessary to effect the German "mission" is illustrated supremely well in the Riezler diary. See the present writer's paper, "Karl Dietrich Erdmann, The Riezler Diary and the Fischer Controversy", p. 250.

[59] Fritz Fischer, "Vom Zaun gebrochen—nicht hineingeschlittert", *Die Zeit*, no. 36, 3 September 1965.

CHAPTER III

The Grasp for World Power

In *War of Illusions* Fischer has narrated the events in Germany which led to war in an unembroidered, non-apologetic style which is, of course, a novelty in German historiography on this subject. It is nonetheless a style and a method which has profound political-pedagogic intent. By revealing the illusions upon which imperial German policy was based Fischer is teaching the new generation of his countrymen that national politics can only be based upon sobriety, rationality and an understanding of the legitimate aspirations of other peoples and not on mystical illusions about one's own national greatness and the decadence of one's neighbours. The illusions which Germans cultivated in 1914 were of the most dangerous character.

The obvious one was that regarding British neutrality. Even as late as the morning of 4 August von Moltke telegraphed to London appealing for sympathetic understanding of the German moves *vis à vis* Belgium because this war was not only concerned with Germany's continued existence as a state but also with the defence and preservation of the Germanic (i.e. Anglo-German) culture against Slavic non-culture.[1]

And further, in spite of the profound disappointment because of the British declaration of war, it was still hoped that Britain would not immediately become an active participant, i.e. send no troops to France because the army would have to be held back for maintaining order in such regions as India, Egypt and Ireland. Indeed, von Moltke had on 2 August indicated that in the event of Britain's entry into the war, subversive activity should be started in India, Egypt and South Africa to stir up anti-British uprisings.

[1] Fischer, *Krieg*, p. 735.

This illusion was coupled with another which expected a number of other states such as Switzerland, Sweden, Norway, Greece, Bulgaria and Rumania to join in on Germany's side. It was hoped that Turkey would begin an offensive against Russia, that Italy would at least remain loyal to the Triple Alliance, that Persia would also rise against Russia and that Japan would exploit Russia's involvement in Europe to expand in the Far East at Russia's expense.

As Fischer comments, this was a truly comprehensive programme which, if realised, would have enveloped the entire world in flames. However, instead of this, all the states in question either reduced or delayed their commitment such as Turkey (until November) or completely refused any whatsoever. Some such as Italy, Rumania, Greece and Sweden, instead of rallying around Germany as the champion of small states, preferred to affirm a strict neutrality and avoid the consequences of association with a Power whose aims and methods were at best somewhat dubious.

The only Power in this depressing list of Germany's dashed hopes which stood by Germany in any meaningful way was Austria-Hungary. But, even here, the latter state was by no means an enthusiastic supporter of German aims. She did not feel compelled to declare war on Russia until 6 August.[2] While Vienna was still trying to prevent Russia from intervening in the Austrian-Serbian conflict (30–31 July) and while under pressure from Britain, Petersburg and Vienna were resuming their talks, the German Kaiser declared on 31 July a situation of threatening war danger and presented ultimata to both Russia and France. On the same afternoon the Kaiser summoned the Austro-Hungarian military attaché (5 p.m.) in order to acquaint him with Germany's efforts to win allies such as Bulgaria, Rumania, Greece, Turkey and Italy.

The purpose of this exercise was to urge Austria to declare war on Russia because Germany would have to direct her main forces against France and only after the defeat of France could Germany mount an offensive against Russia. Again, on

[2] Ibid., p. 737.

the next evening (1 August) the Kaiser repeated these ideas to the Austro-Hungarian ambassador and alluded to the apparently impressive list of allies. The chief aim, the Kaiser revealed, was to bring about a reckoning with France.[3] And to make this possible, Germany pressed Austria to fulfil her duties as an ally in the east and begin immediately a war with Russia.

The Austrian reply to this urging from Berlin was that the declaration of war against Russia was only being postponed to allow Austrian mobilisation in Galicia to proceed undisturbed. But Germany wanted an early, open statement from Austria that Russia had compelled her (Austria) to go to war because of Russian mobilisation against her. Germany maintained that she was forced into war with Russia and France because of Austria; the latter Power ought to recognise this openly.

So there emerged right at the beginning of the war the question of who bore the chief responsibility! It was a latent controversy between the two allies which persisted during the entire war and flared up every time there was a military crisis. However, despite this friction and the English declaration, the German plan to unleash a continental war which had crystallised a month previously through the Sarajevo murder, was fully realised. Only the constellation of forces against the Central Powers was unexpected. Contrary to the hopes of the German leadership, cultivated over recent decades, the smaller Powers did not rally around Germany in the hour of the great "decisive struggle" but sought to preserve their independence by maintaining a wait-and-see-neutrality. Nevertheless, what was not achieved diplomatically in that tense first week of August was to become one of the important war-aims of the German government — a unified Central Europe under German leadership.[4]

As Fischer explained in the "first book", the German blueprint for the future of Europe is to be found in Bethmann Hollweg's September Programme of 1914. It is Fischer's contention that this programme is really the end result of a number of German programmes and conceptions about the

[3] Ibid., p. 738.
[4] Ibid.

new order for Europe — "a war-aims conception of the middle
line". By this Fischer means that the Chancellor was the
recipient of a variety of war-aims-programmes from many
interest groups and that he had to reconcile and reduce them
to practicable, politically attainable and realistic goals. The
programmes came in the shape of formal memoranda through
official channels or in private conversation with government
members or even through the press in public discussion.
Actually, the government itself gave the signal for a veritable
war-aims movement when the Chancellor stated before the
Reichstag that it was Germany's envious neighbours which had
unleashed the war against her. So, understandably, the desire
arose to make the Reich so strong on one hand and to weaken
the enemy on the other that Germany would be secure against
the possibility of attack for all future time.[6] It was natural, with
this understanding of the outbreak of the war that all influential
groups and parties were reflecting on the future position of
Germany in Europe and the world at the termination of a
victorious war. And it was also natural that the plans which
were forged should be based on the conceptions and goals of
pre-war policy because now there was real possibility of being
able to achieve these goals rapidly and on the best possible
terms for Germany. And these pre-war aims were: the destruction of the *Entente*, the expulsion of the Russian colossus from
Central and Eastern Europe, and at least the recognition by
Britain of a new German position of power in the world at large.

The discussion of how all this (the basic conditions for
security and guarantees) was to be achieved, encompassed the
entire range of interest groups, political parties, industrialists,
bankers, national agitators and, of course, members of the
Imperial Government itself. Fischer reveals systematically the
growth of a variety of war-aims-programmes such as those of
the Pan-Germans, the conservatives and the Rhenish-
Westphalian industrialists, all of whose ideas were stamped with
the same conceptions. Their prime concern was with weakening

[5] Ibid., p. 765.
[6] Ibid., p. 753.

France's industrial potential through annexation of vital regions. Russia's face must be forcefully turned eastward and that nation returned essentially to the borders of Peter the Great. It is not difficult here to detect the pre-war "Berlin-Baghdad ideology".[7]

Similar goals, formulated before the war, were expressed formally in the first weeks of hostilities by leading party officials and members of the *Reichstag* such as Matthias Erzberger of the Centre Party. Others, such as bankers, exporters and many intellectuals were not so enthusiastic about an annexationist programme as with achieving a rapid victory and imposing commercial treaties on the vanquished nations in the form of a continental customs union which would keep them effectively within the German orbit.

Even the "moderate" parties and the Social Democrats had their ideas for gaining security for German power within Europe. In particular the Social Democrats were concerned with the elimination of the Russian threat. They were indeed successful in mobilising the working class in the struggle against Czarism, a fact which gave the Social Democrats a common goal with the most conservative and reactionary forces. Of sourse, the socialist leaders and trade union bosses were aware of this and hoped to use their loyalty to national goals in order to extract constitutional concessions from the government.[8]

All this discussion early in the war was essentially an enthusiastic refurbishing and reformulation of ideas and policies which had germinated and taken shape in the preceding decades. They cannot be regarded as *ad hoc* solutions to totally new problems thrown up by the outbreak of war; rather the war cleared the way for the more efficient realisation of these goals. Fischer explains how these goals were crystallised:

> *Mitteleuropa* and *Mittelafrika* were in August and early September the war aims which formed . . . the central complex of the war-aims policies of the German government, the bourgeois parties and the economic associations. Between and within the various groups there were admittedly many divergencies; however, all streams had in common the great goal, after a victorious war, so to shape the

[7] Ibid., p. 741.   [8] Ibid., p. 751.

position of the German Reich that it would be for foreseeable time impregnable against any enemy coalition. The way to this solution—and this goal was common to the most influential groups and the Reich Chancellor—was the extension of the German power position on the Continent. *Mitteleuropa* under German leadership appeared to offer the best guarantee to permit Germany to rise to become the fourth world power if not the leading power on earth. Indeed, Riezler went so far as to speak of German "world domination".[9]

The essential thing about the September Programme is that it is a compromise, an expression of Bethmann's earlier enunciated policy of diagonals. In short, it is a compromise between the extremists among the military, the Pan-German League and certain ruthless industrialists on one hand who demanded extensive annexation of enemy territory and those "moderates" who saw in annexations the seeds of future uprisings (neo-Rankean caution?).[10] This latter group which included the Chancellor himself preferred the establishment of a large central European economic unit which would permit Germany to maintain herself in competition with the British Empire, the U.S.A., Russia, Japan and China.[11] Naturally, the achievement of this latter plan presumed a total victory also which would enable Germany to dictate terms of peace.

The Chancellor's programme which was tabled on 9 September 1914 at a point when the military victory appeared within easy grasp, bore the title "Preliminary Directives for our Policy at the Conclusion of Peace".[12] It allowed for both annexations and the establishment of a central European customs union. The first part states the overall aim:

> Security for the German Reich towards west and east for imaginable time. For this purpose France must be so weakened that she cannot re-emerge as a great Power. Russia to be forced back from the German border where possible and her domination over the non-Russian tributary peoples broken.[13]

The second part elaborates the details of how this was to be achieved. France was to be made economically dependent upon

[9] Ibid., p. 765.
[10] Ibid., p. 772. c.f. Anneliese Thimme, *Hans Delbrück als Kritiker der Wilhelminischen Epoche*, p. 117.
[11] Ibid., p. 771.   [12] Ibid., p. 767.   [13] Ibid., p. 768.

Germany having to forfeit the iron ore region of Briey and forced into a commercial treaty which would turn France into an exclusively German market. Belgium was to be similarly treated and transformed into a tributary state which allowed the German use of her channel ports. Luxemburg was to become a part of the German Federation.

Further, there was the demand to unite all the lands in the west (France, Belgium and Holland) plus those in the north (Denmark and possibly Sweden and Norway) plus the south (possibly into a central European customs union – the core of the *Mitteleuropa* concept).

> The foundations of a central European economic unit through a common tariff agreement is to be achieved . . . This unit, presumably without a common constitutional point with apparent equality of privilege for the members, but really under German leadership, must stabilise the economic predominance of Germany over Central Europe.[14]

The question of *Mittelafrika* as a colonial aim was made contingent on the achievement of the *Mitteleuropa* aim, so there were no precise details elaborated. The same was true for Russia:

> The question of colonial acquisitions under which in the first place the creation of a unified central African colonial empire is to be achieved, likewise the aims to be realised in Russia, will be examined later.[15]

That this programme represented a compromise on the part of the Chancellor is evidenced by the fact that he was severely criticised by extremists for not going far enough! However, it remained in essence the government's programme throughout the war despite the efforts of heavy industry, the East Elbian agriculturalists and most of the generals to expand it into a programme of naked annexation. In this light the programme is a supreme example of how foreign policy is in fact dictated by the outcome of the domestic political infighting. The fact was that Bethmann's apparent moderation was considered weak-

[14] Ibid., p. 769.
[15] Ibid.

ness in many influential quarters. Therefore, the Chancellor had
to struggle very hard to keep a working majority for his policy
within the *Reichstag* as well as the Prussian Diet, cabinet and
military circles. Finally, Bethmann was dropped in July 1917;
his policy of diagonals no longer suited the ruling social groups
who convinced the Supreme Army Command under Hinden-
burg and Ludendorff that Bethmann Hollweg's ideas no longer
coincided with those of the nation.[16]

Despite the relative moderation of Bethmann's concepts it
will have become evident that the goals he maintained were
the product not only of Germany's continental position but
more particularly of a unique German ideology of the state.
Kurt Riezler's pen has provided sufficient evidence for this.
And while one may recognise the tragedy of Bethmann's position in the hotbed of extremists and appreciate his efforts of
statesmanship, one is impressed all the more by the power of
ideas which "possess" men. Bethmann, as were his extremist
critics, was convinced of the rightness of Germany's world
historical mission, namely that Europe had to be re-organised
under German leadership. All were agreed that the pre-
condition for this was a rapid German victory in the west which
would then free sufficient troops to enable an equally decisive
victory in the east. Everything, armaments, technology and
economic preparation, was geared to this end. However, the
"short purifying storm" which Bethmann had expected proved
to be an illusion. The hope that the war would last at the
most four months was vain. The order of 10 September to
German troops to withdraw after the loss of the Battle of the
Marne signified the failure of the planned *Blitzkrieg* and the
beginning of a four year long world war for which Germany
was not prepared.

This fact was recognised not only by Bethmann but also by
the Army. Falkenhayn, von Moltke's successor, had confided
to Erzberger that the war was really lost after the failure of
the first Marne offensive. In December 1914 the same general
expressed the opinion that the German army after such severe

16 Ibid., p. 774.

losses had become a "shattered instrument".[17] But having
made this observation the German leaders failed to draw the
logical conclusion that with a shattered army no decision could
be forced in the west. Here another German illusion was burst,
namely that the French and British forces would not offer
serious resistance; the French and British counter-attack across
the entire front on 6 September came as a complete and sober-
ing surprise.[18]

Nevertheless, as Fischer illustrates, the illusion survived that
Germany could force France and Britain to their knees and
dictate a peace treaty on the terms already outlined. Bethmann
Hollweg himself, however, soon became aware that the entire
programme could not be achieved. The earliest alternatives
were to make a separate peace in either east or west and only
pursue the war in one direction or, on the other hand to continue fighting to the point of exhaustion of all sides and make
a peace on the basis of the *status quo*. In the first case, the
chance of a partial realisation of goals seemed a possibility; in
the second all one would achieve was the satisfaction of know-
ing that such a great coalition was unable to force the German
Reich to its knees. But as Bethmann Hollweg realised, neither
of these alternatives would have appealed to the nation; it
would appear as insufficient reward for such enormous sacri-
fice.[19]

For these reasons, then, the Chancellor was reluctant to
divulge to the nation the real significance of the military re-
versals at the Marne and Ypres. In this way he kept up morale
on the home front (fighting-spirit and will to persevere) but by
doing so the Chancellor unwittingly caused an intensification of
the political and economic demands of the influential pressure
groups. And these, of course, in view of the real capacity of
the forces in the field became more and more unrealistic. Because of this the Chancellor could not bring himself to tell the
writers of war-aims memoranda the unpalatable military facts.
Bethmann's dilemma was that on one hand he had to assure
the annexationists that the war would not be terminated until

[17] Ibid., p. 778.   [18] Ibid., p. 775.   [19] Ibid., p. 779.

Germany had achieved an impregnable position, while on the other hand he had to emphasise the defensive character of the war to the Social Democrats. He, therefore, attempted to resolve the situation by claiming that Germany was fighting for "security and guarantees".

This formula, however, failed in the end to placate the powerful conservative and chauvinistic elements within Germany who increasingly wished to see the war aims extended to ever more unrealistic proportions. The main fear of these groups was of making peace prematurely and thus squandering the great advantages so dearly purchased. It was because of these illusions that the war to establish German hegemony in the world was continued for four years when actually it had been lost between September and November 1914. Admittedly the allies formed a war pact on 4 September 1914 in which they each gave assurances not to make a separate peace with Germany and therefore the possibility of shortening the war was destroyed. However, be that as it may, from the German point of view the duration of the war was the result of both the tenacity with which the political and economic leaders believed in the future position of Germany in the world and of their conviction that only a victorious war could guarantee their own social and political position within the Reich.[20]

Seldom have the illusory conceptions of a nation's "historical role" generated such superhuman tenacity and fanatical conviction with such dire results. The significance of Fritz Fischer's work for Germans lies in their recognition of this fact. By coming to terms with their past through the help of such frank and courageous teachers Germans are creating the ideological-political pre-condition for a durable democratic order in central Europe. So are the implications of the Fischer revolution in German historiography of more than ephemeral relevance. As one of the more perceptive German critics has remarked:

> The two German wars of the twentieth century were above all wars of illusions because they rested on anachronistic concepts, viz. that in order to be great a country had to embark upon military con-

[20] Ibid., p. 783.

quest. Unfortunately the anachronistic illusions upon which these wars were based have still not died out. That Fischer has ruthlessly exposed them is his greatest merit. The reading of his book causes the scales to fall from one's eyes: the entire body of ideas on which the two German wars rested was wrong; sixty million people died because of an error of logic. In revealing this error Fischer's book not only relates history; it *makes* history.[21]

[21] Sebastian Haffner, "Befreiende Wahrheit", *Konkret*, 11 December 1969, p. 55.

CHAPTER IV

"What the Fuss was about"

The title of this chapter is taken from a *Times Literary Supplement* review article in which among other works on Germany the "Fischer Festschrift" was examined. The writer stated that the Fischer controversy was "beginning to look very old fashioned. It is not altogether easy to see what the fuss was about".[1] The bored disdain with which the British writer affects to regard the Fischer controversy indicates that propinquity is no guarantee of familiarity with the essence of what is going on. Dare one venture to assert or even suggest what the fuss was about, the fuss which the presumably donnish writer of the *TLS* review finds so hard to comprehend? It is admittedly very difficult for highly civilised persons serenely encapsulated in their trim-lawned, gothic colleges to appreciate what savage passions were surging through the monarchical-martial breasts of the late Professor Gerhard Ritter and his army of outraged German patriots who took up cudgels against the sensation-seeking nest-fouling Fischer school. The fact is that there has been an unusually vehement dispute among German scholars over Professor Fischer's books. It has endured at least since 1961 and is only now beginning to diminish with Fischer having defended his position against all comers. A "fuss" of this nature lasting over ten years in a country like Germany deserves more attention than the *TLS* reviewer obviously had time or inclination to devote to it.

In Britain, academic disputes are not usually taken seriously by a very wide circle. When a Leavis pillories a Snow, or an A. J. P. Taylor quarrels with a Trevor-Roper, it has no political or social significance whatever. The spleen of the dons directed

[1] "War Heroes", *Times Literary Supplement,* 31 August 1973. p. 1006.

at each other, interests no one but themselves. Fellow academics
are either slightly amused or a little shocked at the lack of
charity displayed by such otherwise cultured and in some
cases reputedly Christian men. But in Germany the scholars are
not so isolated from political life as in Britain, though at first
glance the reverse might rather appear to have been the case.
To put it in a "very German way", in Britain the professors
did not and do not exercise the same formative influence on
the general political will as their German colleagues were wont
to do. Perhaps this was because in Britain, no large body of
history professors could be sufficiently stirred up to care under
what brand of regime they lived so long as academic life could
go on in a more or less tolerable fashion. This would of course
presume the existence of a regime in favour of academic freedom. One could observe that political stability was of such a
relatively high order anyway that there was no need for
academics to emerge as champions for this or that political
solution to the nation's problems. This of course is not to deny
that certain academics with political vision and a social conscience were not very actively trying to influence the course of
politics.[2] However, there was no school or tradition of political
historians to compare with that which emerged in Germany in
the nineteenth century — the school which no less a person than
Acton himself investigated.[3] The Germans, as has been seen,
were a vastly different breed of scholars. They enjoyed a
"mandarin" status, as Fritz Ringer has recently stressed, and
were vitally concerned not so much with the minutae of day
to day issues but with the long term direction and posture of
national politics, and the preservation of the social-political
order. They were at pains to bolster up what they regarded as
the historically evolved Bismarckian constitution and the

[2] Perhaps the most notable British historian to exert an influence on
politics was Sir John Robert Seeley (1834–1895). See Adolf Rein, *Sir
John Robert Seeley*. Examples of more recent academic and ideological
influence on political decision-making in Britain are to be found in
A. J. P. Taylor, *The Trouble Makers*.

[3] Lord Acton, "German Schools of History", *EHR* I (1886).

assumptions upon which it rested. When that construction collapsed and was replaced by one based on foreign, Western and republican principles they were thrown into a confusion of seemingly hopeless nostalgia. On surveying the ruins of their country after 1918 they perceived their task essentially as a politically restorative one.

It is very well known that the majority of German historians during the Weimar period had no real loyalty to the republic. At the best, they became like Friedrich Meinecke, "republicans by reason" (*Vernunftrepublikaner*) and remained monarchists at heart (*Herzensmonarchisten*).[4] As a group which could have contributed enormously to modernising the political consciousness of at least the student generation, the body of German historians of the Weimar period failed miserably. The memory of this failure is very evident in the work of the present generation of German historians – due in no small degree to Fritz Fischer. In the Weimar period, as has been noted, the German historians perceived their dominating task in trying to repudiate the war guilt accusation of Versailles.

The posthumously famous Eckart Kehr noted that the impact of the Great War and the change-over to a republican government had very little effect on the political outlook and basic methodological assumptions of the German historians.[5] There neither occurred a social-political re-orientation of any consequence nor a detachment from inherited scholarly traditions. Although there was much talk and some writing about the crisis of historicism, "historiographical practice and its historical premises were scarcely affected".[6] Indeed, the political behaviour of the professional historians reflected the overall

[4] c.f. Imanuel Geiss, "Kritischer Rückblick auf Friedrich Meinecke", in *Studien zur Geschichte und Geschichtswissenschaft*, p. 96.

[5] c.f. Eckart Kehr, "Neuere deutsche Geschichtsschreibung", in *Der Primat der Innenpolitik*, p. 266, and Bernd Faulenbach, "Deutsche Geschichtswissenschaft zwischen Kaiserreich und NS—Diktatur", in *Geschichtswissenschaft in Deutschland*, p. 84.

[6] Faulenbach, "Deutsche Geschichtswissenschaft . . . ", pp. 84–85. See the major works reflecting on historism by Ernst Troeltsch, Karl Heussi and Friedrich Meinecke.

fact that the liberal-parliamentary experiment of Weimar in the final analysis broke on the resistance of the majority of the old ruling élite of Prusso-Germany. And, again as Kehr had observed, this élite was morally sustained, aided and abetted by the German academics.[7]

Just how questionable the political-social and methodological tradition of German historians was, can be deduced from their behaviour during the Third Reich. The year 1933 signified no dramatic caesura in the trends within German historiography. It continued largely as if unaffected by the momentous transformation in the state. What is most significant is that although no occupants of professorial chairs of history in 1933 were National Socialists, the profession did not have to be "co-ordinated" (*gleichgeschaltet*) by the new regime as were institutions which were considered incompatible with the aims of the Nazis.[8] There occurred what has been called a voluntary co-ordination of the academics (*freiwillige Gleichschaltung*).[9] And after 1933 there were "astonishingly few collisions between that which the Nazi regime represented and expected and that which was taught and written by the historians".[10]

As Berd Faulenbach notes, the limitations of a historiography which was oriented to an anachronistic system of values rather than to the social problems of the present and future are more than obvious.[11] However, it was not only the historians' Prusso-German monarchical nostalgia which militated against the

[7] Kehr, "Neuere deutsche Geschichtsschreibung", pp. 260 and 266.

[8] The German noun "Gleichschaltung" as employed with reference to the Third Reich is best rendered by "co-ordination". In practice it meant the process of incorporating all institutions within the orbit of National Socialist ideology and organisation. For the behaviour of the history professors see Manfred Schlenke, "Geschichtsdeutung und Selbstverständnis im 19. und 20. Jahrhundert" in *Haltungen und Fehlhaltungen in Deutschland,* ed. Hermann Glaser, pp. 78–87, and Karl Ferdinand Werner, *Das NS—Geschichtsbild.*

[9] c.f. Karl Otmar Freiherr von Aretin, "Die Deutsche Universität im Dritten Reich" in *FH* XXIII, no. 10 (1968), pp. 689–696.

[10] Rolf Vierhaus, "Walter Frank und die Geschichtswissenschaft" in *HZ* CCVII (1968), p. 619.

[11] Faulenbach, "Deutsche Geschichtswissenschaft . . . ", p. 85.

flourishing of a modern parliamentary democracy in Germany, but also the coincidence of the conservative historians' aims with those of the Nazis.[12]

This state of affairs constituted an enormous embarrassment for the majority of German history professors after 1945 because they generally survived the Third Reich in office. This fact alone pointed to an obvious moral collapse of German scholarship. Against their presumably better judgment they accepted Hitler, maintained a cowardly silence or behaved opportunistically.[13] However, with the liberation of Germany from the Nazi tyranny these scholars made only superficial or tentative attempts at revising their image of Prusso-German history.[14] Only in the 'sixties, affirms Karl Ferdinand Werner, did a really searching historical analysis begin. As he puts the painful question: Did Hitler's successes take place really against the better judgment of the scholars and were these accepted only out of weakness of character? Professor Werner now points to the pioneering significance of the Fischer school in contributing clarity on these questions, and that against the resistance of many colleagues. Regardless of one's attitude to the over-dramatised war-guilt question which Fischer re-awakened, he forced German historians to make two harrowing inferences:[15]

(1) The Weimar period and long before that, Imperial Germany, scarcely represented states of innocence from which Germany was torn by Hitler and his barbarians.

(2) Hitler's world of ideas and that of his supporters was formed to such an extent before 1914 that here is explained not only where Hitler got them from but also why he was so successful with the German masses.

[12] c.f. the present writer's paper, "The Crisis in West German Historiography—Origins and Trends" in *HS* VIII (1969).

[13] Karl Ferdinand Werner, "Deutsche Historiographie unter Hitler" in *Geschichtswissenschaft in Deutschland,* ed. Bernd Faulenbach, p. 87.

[14] Perhaps the best known examples (in English) at revision are the essays collected by Hans Kohn (see bibliography) and Ludwig Dehio's *Germany and World Politics in the Twentieth Century.*

[15] Werner, "Deutsche Historiographie . . . ", p. 87.

Research on the German universities and especially the historians whose writings were expressions of political thinking before and during the Hitler period indicates that the professors and teachers cultivated ideas concerning the state and nationalism which coincided with the core of Nazi doctrine. This, says Werner, indicates not so much a moral collapse of scholarship but rather an intellectual collapse. In this regard the historians were particularly culpable because they contributed to the creation and propagation of concepts (if not of completely racist character, then closely allied thereto) *before* they were compelled or felt compelled to do so. It was this attitude which made any attempt by the Nazis to "co-ordinate" the universities either superfluous or difficult. It would have appeared ridiculous for the Nazis to move against "well-meaning", "nationally minded" and "reliable" academics. Furthermore, their resistance to the Nazis in the sphere of their formal scholarly teaching and research was all the more successful because the Nazis could offer no alternative. They themselves could not have supplied academic replacements in sufficient numbers to keep the universities functioning.

This is an interesting situation because with the "liberation" of 1945 another kind of co-ordination took place, this time in a presumably democratic direction. But could one assume that because the Nazi tyranny had been replaced by a new order imposed by the Western allies that the German professors still in office had suddenly changed their inner convictions? Werner draws attention to the most recent research in West Germany carried out by a group of younger historians under the guidance of Professor Hans-Ulrich Wehler on the former (i.e. now deceased) history professors in Germany. This work has shown that the older generations of historians functioned as representatives and spokesmen of the upper middle class who were established in positions of power in the administration, economy as well as cultural life.[16] Werner asserts that this class was

[16] See Wehler's five-volume edition of essays by various younger German historians in bibliography. c.f. Werner, "Deutsche Historiographie . . . ". p. 88.

willing to maintain itself against all threats from other classes by using any means at its disposal! This included supporting aggressive external policies in order to divert the masses from any attack on their own position. To this extent, this "ruling class" was in reality better represented (than one had previously assumed) by the Kaiser and even Hitler whom they damned only *after his failure* (emphasis added). These people could, of course, maintain that they acted in good faith to defend the traditional values of the fatherland as loyal German patriots. And subjectively from their own view point they were indeed that. However, an objective social analysis and recognition of this subjective moral consciousness provides the clue, accord· ing to Werner, to understanding the otherwise virtually mystifying history of Germany between 1914 and 1945.[17]

Echoing Fischer's *War of Illusions,* Professor Werner puts his finger on the neuralgic point when he characterises the disappointment of the German middle classes after 1918. Their dreams of world power had then been brutally shattered only to be followed by years of economic hardship. This they interpreted as the result of the evil machinations of a world of enemies both within as well as without who deceived the nation of its rightful place in the world. It was this state of mind which pre-disposed the Germans to accept Hitler and his virulent anti-semitism. In addition to this psychosis of despair, Werner mentions the German sense of wounded pride and superiority.[18] The long tradition of cultural excellence since Goethe, the Prussian military successes of the nineteenth century plus the rapid economic growth during the Bismarckian-Wilhelmine empire resulted in the firm belief in the superiority of German efficiency which only lacked the right kind of leadership in order to prove to the world again the fact of German superiority.[19]

In this tradition lived a considerable number of German history professors, even if many of them believed they stood above such over-simplified modes of thought. As Werner correctly observes, the spectrum ranged from a relatively liberal

[17] Ibid.   [18] Ibid., p. 89.   [19] Ibid.

but still strongly nationalist upper bourgeois mentality of a Friedrich Meinecke and his numerous pupils, to a pronounced nationalist, extremely conservative or even racialist viewpoint such as represented by an Adalbert Wahl or a Karl Alexander von Müller.[20] It is, then, not surprising that they felt themselves uncomfortable in the militarily humiliated and economically unstable Weimar Republic. In this regard they were predisposed to make straight the path for a new saviour.[21] In drawing attention to the intellectual preparation for the First World War by the historians and by implication for the advent of Hitler, Fritz Fischer has done more than any other German historian not only to revise the national historical image but also to indict the fabricators and sustainers of that image. That, in short, is what the fuss has been about. Only with this in mind is it possible to appreciate the political-ideological motivation of the works of the late Gerhard Ritter, of the series of polemics against the Fischer school, of the apologetics of Professors Erdmann, Hillgruber, W. J. and H. Mommsen, Gustav Schmidt as well as many others. K. F. Werner maintains that perhaps the most important result of the entire Fischer controversy is that it has laid bare the mentality of Germany's intellectual and political élite both prior to and during the First World War.[22] This has served as the basis for their stance during the Weimar Republic and explains their subsequent (qualified) approval of the Hitler dictatorship.

In order to highlight the reasons for the "fuss" it will suffice to outline the major criticisms levelled at Fischer. When all the smoke cleared away it could be seen that there were only two

[20] Ibid. Adalbert Wahl (1871–1957) was a professor at the University of Tübingen 1910–1938. Karl Alexander von Müller (1882–1964) was a professor in Munich 1917–1945. He was also the first German Rhodes Scholar, and is now chiefly remembered for editing the prestigious *Historische Zeitschrift* from 1935 to 1945.

[21] Werner, "Deutsche Historiographie . . . ", p. 89. Here Professor Werner traces how the historians during the 'twenties paved the way for a take-over by a strong man by founding a virtual cult of admiration for the great German political and military heroes of the past.

[22] Ibid., footnote no. 2, p. 179.

aspects which aroused the ire of the critics. These were Fischer's account of the July crisis (i.e. war guilt) and his treatment of the Chancellor, Bethmann Hollweg. The old-guard history professors led by Gerhard Ritter were incensed at the Fischer version of the July crisis simply because it exploded their "encirclement theory" and consequently destroyed the validity of any thesis suggesting that Germany only went to war in 1914 for defensive reasons. Fischer, like Kantorowicz before him, has shown beyond doubt (especially in *War of Illusions*) that Germany had no grounds to fear attack from neighbouring Powers; rather it was they who were nervous about German moves.

The implications of this for the attitude and behaviour of German historians towards the lost 1914–1918 war, the November revolution, the "stab-in-the-back" theory, Versailles, reparations and the rise of Hilter are profound. The paradigm of belief which they had constructed can be summarised as follows: The Reich was encircled by a group of envious, vengeful and barbaric Powers before 1914. This group, the Entente, saw an opportunity in the July 1914 crisis to trap Germany in a war to eliminate her as a competitor in trade and industry (Britain), to win back lost territory (France) and to extend national interest at German expense (Russia). The Reich had only wished to preserve her ally, Austria-Hungary, from collapse. Germany had thus gone to war for the noblest of motives.

When the Reich and her allies were defeated by a world of numerically and materially superior enemies, she was wrongfully accused of having started the war and then forced to accept the harshest treaty conditions imaginable. In addition to this, too, internal enemies of the left had been working for the overthrow of the monarchical order. These had weakened the Reich's power of resistance at the critical time when, if the war could not have been actually won, at least better treaty conditions could have been achieved. The "stab-in-the-back" was therefore a major factor in Germany's subsequent malaise during the Weimar Republic.[23]

[23] Karen Thiessenhusen, "Politische Kommentare deutscher Historiker zur Revolution und Neuordnung 1918/19", *APZ* B45 (1969), pp. 25–34.

The Treaty of Versailles with its accusation of war-guilt, colonial guilt and the infamous reparations conditions was nothing short of the moral and physical humiliation and enslavement of the German nation. Because of the monstrous injustice, the German people in their misery and despair allowed themselves to be deceived by the diabolical Hitler[24] who alone among the German politicians could make good his pledge to liberate the nation from the bondage of Versailles.[25] In this way conservative German apologists could dissociate themselves from the Nazi success in their homeland. Hitler was merely the result of a political miscalculation by a people who were more sinned against than sinning. The dictator could only have come to power as a result of Versailles and the world economic crisis which was in part caused by the vicious reparations system.[26]

This neat paradigm has been totally destroyed by Fischer and so there have had to be more subtle attempts to account for the rise of Adolf Hitler if one is not to see him in the way such historical writers as A. J. P. Taylor, William Shirer or Eduard Vermeil do, namely as relatively normal if somewhat more vigorous exponent of traditional German policies. And this is why Fischer's treatment of Bethmann Hollweg has attracted so much criticism. For the conservative apologists he was the last refuge around whom they could build up an image on an honourable German statesman who was conscientiously trying to preserve the security of his country and was genuinely concerned to preserve world peace. Unfortunately, this manoeuvre, too, has been torpedoed by the Fischer school.

[24] c.f. the assessments of Hitler by Karl Dietrich Erdmann in vol. IV of Bruno Gebhardt, *Handbuch der Deutschen Geschichte,* p. 185, and by Ludwig Dehio, *Germany and World Politics in the Twentieth Century,* p. 32.

[25] c.f. the present writer's article, "The Crisis in West German Historiography—Origins and Trends", p. 458.

[26] This is the burden of a number of German works purporting to explain the advent of Hitler. See the present writer's "Hitler between Prussianism and Mass Hysteria—Some Post-War German Views", in *Historical Journal* (University of Newcastle/Australia).

Initially, the reaction to Fischer's portrayal of Bethmann's statesmanship took three forms, as Arnold Sywottek has reported:[27]

(1) The new facts provided by Fischer might or might not give cause to revise the traditional image of Bethmann.

(2) The documented statements by Bethmann may indeed be authentic but they contradict the "character" and "nature" of the man.

(3) The newly discovered facts indicate hitherto unknown inclinations and personality traits in Bethmann and demand a reinvestigation of the political structure and context (Zusammenhang) of his chancellorship.

Historians who took the first line were trying by the application of an exaggerated scepticism to retain the above outlined paradigm of "encirclement leading to Nazi dictatorship". They were unwilling to revise the paradigm because of the uncomfortable light it would throw on their behaviour and attitudes during the Weimar Republic and Third Reich. Those who took the second line were, of course, trying to flee into a realm which, because of the irrational subjective component, cannot be the basis of any scholarly discussion. The third line of approach was at least productive of attempts at rational enquiry, and some highly impressive works have emerged since Fischer's pioneering efforts which analyse in great detail the power structure and tendencies of Wilhelmine Germany. Whether or not these have "corrected" the findings of the Fischer-Geiss research is very doubtful.

In this regard, the massive work of Professor Dieter Groh deserves mention because he has made full use of Fischer's findings and method and comes to conclusions which only modify Fischer by a nuance.[28] However, for Groh the nuance is of critical importance. He states that Germany bore the main guilt but not the sole guilt for the outbreak of the First World War and attributes Germany's war-like policies as being due to an increasing willingness to resort to what Groh calls a

[27] Arnold Sywottek, "Die Fischer Kontroverse", p. 30.
[28] Dieter Groh, Negative Integration und revolutionärer Attentismus.

preventive war. This *Präventivkriegsbereitschaft* came from fear, not from any irrational lust to conquer. The fear was of a dual nature. First, there was anxiety regarding the upsurge of democratic forces inside Germany which threatened the conservative-monarchical-feudal order. Second, there was anxiety regarding the expansionist tendencies of Russia who would, if left to grow, completely frustrate German foreign policy aspirations for the future. It was these dual fears which caused Germany to attempt in July–August 1914 to establish domestic stability and at the same time ensure her external freedom of movement for years to come by defeating Russia, France and Britain in a Blitzkrieg in 1914. So it was not aggressive tendencies on Germany's part but essentially motives of self-preservation. These may have appeared to the outside world as aggressive but on closer examination Germany's motives were defensive.[29]

Here we have at least an example of German historiography which has recognised the inescapable need to investigate structures and tendencies as well as the biography of the decision-making statesman. But whereas other critics of Fischer have recognised the need to abandon the traditional *Historismus* approach and investigate structural factors as well, they still try to carp at Fischer.

Gustav Schmidt for example has mounted a frontal attack on the entire Fischer school by denying that German war aims emerged from the socio-political power structure of the Wilhelmine Reich. In his analysis of the Reich constitution he puts the question whether or not the possession of power and influence is really identical with governing.[30] Schmidt would like to know who or what group at a given point in time was actually exercising power and influence over the government. In his examination of the shifting party alliances in the *Reichstag* (*Blockbildung*) Schmidt wants to show that although they were potentially influential they tended to cancel each other out in end effect. Therefore, they exercised no determining influence

---

[29] Ibid., pp. 618–652.
[30] Gustav Schmidt, "Innenpolitsche Blockbildung am Vorabend des Ersten Weltkrieges" in *APZ* B20 (1972), p. 4.

on the Reich government. Under these circumstances it would be absurd to argue that influential pressure groups or political parties, no matter of what ideological persuasion, could have had any effect on ultimate policy decisions. As Imanuel Geiss has commented, this process of mutual frustration helps explain why the Reich constitution remained so inflexible and unable to reform itself in a parliamentary direction. However, it does not to any degree serve to repudiate Fischer. The Reich government still did not rule in a vacuum isolated from socio-economic and political forces. Bethmann Hollweg's own admission of pursuing a policy of diagonals is sufficient to refute that.[31] In short, Schmidt's attempt to discredit Fischer by trying to show that the various parties in the *Reichstag* neutralised each other's potential to influence policy is a methodological red-herring. He has made a great deal of "fuss" to no avail. How is it possible to assume that decision-making statesmen are unaffected by the prevailing pressures and ideologies and that instead they make their policies with reference to some ideal formula handed down through the ages? The "fuss" that Schmidt has made is only explainable in terms of a curious nostalgia (i.e. curious for one born in 1938) for the ethos of past epoch, the virtues of which he would like to see preserved in the present. It is also an attitude determined by a certain myopia for political realities on one hand and a misplaced patriotism on the other, i.e. a patriotism which will not admit that the First World War emerged out of the failure of the German Reich to modernise its constitution.[32]

A similar example of a young German professor's stubborn refusal to concede that the Fischer school has "hit the nail on the head" with regard to its interpretation of the causes of the First World War is Wolfgang J. Mommsen (born 1930). He

[31] Geiss, "Die Fischerkontroverse . . . ", p. 187, c.f. Hans Günter Zmarzlik, *Bethmann Hollweg als Reichskanzler.*

[32] c.f. Fritz Stern, *The Failure of Illiberalism,* p. xxvii: "Illiberalism heightened the fitful recklessness of Germany's disastrous policy in it— until the very external policy that was intended to save the illiberal society brought about its seeming destruction through the defeat of November 1918."

has published numerous articles not only in German but also in British and American journals virtually all with the aim of weakening Fischer's position as has been seen. His latest effort continues to deny that despite the admittedly large German share in causing the First World War it was not the result of an unrestrained lust for power, but rather of internal weaknesses and confusion within the inner circles of the ruling élite of the Reich.[33] The tensions and divisions within that group resulted in foreign policy calculations which to a remarkably high degree were dependent on the moves of third Powers, especially Russia and Austria-Hungary.[34] This minimising of the aggressive component in the German power élite juxtaposed with an emphasis on the internal constitutional crises and instability is, like Gustav Schmidt's work, helpful up to a point. One is bound to have a greater sympathy for the dilemma of the central decision-makers. However, none of this in any way weakens Fischer's position. The latter has in *War of Illusions* indicated very fully that he appreciates the internal crises of the Reich. Indeed, Fischer is asserting that the Reich foreign policy was an expression of internal tensions. One of his main points is surely that it was the Reich's failure to resolve those domestic tensions that led to the reckless forward foreign policy.

If, since the death of Gerhard Ritter, the Fischer opponents have recognised the validity of Fischer's main assertions, then one may legitimately enquire why do they still refuse to acknowledge the merits of his work? No one who is not a cynical nationalist can in all conscience reverse what Fischer has done, since facts are facts. Nevertheless, one perceives that his achievements are only grudgingly recognised. The now sobered critics have woken up to the fact that the Fischer school have left very little vulnerable area against which they can mount serious attacks. So the "fuss" is dying down, though

[33] Wolfgang J. Mommsen, "Die latente Krise des Wilhelminischen Reiches. Staat und Gesellschaft in Deutschland 1890–1914", in *MGM* XV (1974), pp. 7–28.
[34] Ibid., p. 28.

with bad grace on the part of some. They have had to realise that there are very few Prusso-German values fit to be preserved. By pointing this out Fischer has created the precondition for Germany's moral as distinct from economic integration into Western Europe. This he has done by destroying the old Prussian-dominated image of German history and all that this implied. But this was done not out of an iconoclastic lust for destruction but rather, as Helmut Lindemann observed, out of patriotic concern. Fischer's work is an appeal to Germans to revise not only their historical image but their political values.[35] It has taken, understandably, a little time to achieve this because a political tradition which goes back to Frederick the Great via Treitschke, Bismarck, Ranke and Hegel could not be remoulded without some degree of "fuss".

CHAPTER V

The End of Statism in German Historiography

It will remain for future generations to assess the full impact of Fischer's historiographical achievement. Nothing short of a new totalitarian seizure of power in West Germany could possibly erase the effect, already perceptible, which this new style of history is having upon the younger generation of students. The open debate, the clinically critical methodology and the total rejection of national apologetics by the Fischer-school had contributed enormously to the sweeping away of emotional barriers to an objective reappraisal of this nation's recent past. Above all, Fischer's many-sided analysis of the various factors influencing the formulation of German policy has taught Germans the fallacy of regarding politics, both domestic and international, as the Olympian preserve of one great man. It has taught them that even in a state such as Bismarckian-Wilhelmine Germany, the decision-making process was highly complex and the end-product of many pressures operating about the centre of power. Government was scarcely a matter of a cool calculation of *raison d'état* by the highest officials made in isolation from the rivalries and intrigues of powerful interest groups. The old Bismarck historiography had contributed much to sustaining that myth about the formulation of high policy. In addition, Fischer has shown his countrymen how, during the days of the monarchy, powerful individuals made reckless and irrational decisions with far-reaching and disastrous consequences, and that these decisions were based upon largely chimerical assumptions.

The lessons for the present and future generation of historians which Fischer has taught is that national history must have three dimensions to it. The old statist tradition which merely

concerned itself with the political and military leadership of the
nation is only one dimension, and on its own is clearly inadequate. The central actors in the drama have to be placed in
the social and economic fabric of their time and this adds the
second and tremendously important dimension which has
hitherto been neglected in Germany. As Wolfgang J. Mommsen
has noted:

> . . . the political and social structure of society and its various
> organisational forms as well as its imminent trends begin to interest
> scholars more than the motives of statesmen and leading person-
> alities.[1]

All this, of course, had been recognised by other leading
historians after 1945 and even before. Men such as Theodor
Schieder in Cologne and Werner Conze in Heidelberg had
certainly been very concerned with the *structure* of society in
a given epoch as they set out to analyse changes in that structure as well as to explain the motives of the leading actors on
the historical stage. However, these men, despite their sincere
rejection of the Third Reich, were, as Georg Iggers comments,
still deeply rooted in the nationalist school, i.e.

> On the one hand they are much more able to see the German
> national state in its manifold historical perspective but on the other
> hand they are still deeply committed to the national and idealistic
> tradition.[2]

Fischer has clearly broken with that tradition and this explains why his anti-nationalist tendency has earned him so
much criticism from many of his eminent colleagues. His third
dimension to national historiography is the ideological one. His
research has been undertaken from a standpoint which only a
very few isolated individualists previously had ventured to
adopt.[3] Although Fischer was trained in the historicist school,

---

[1] Wolfgang J. Mommsen, "Historical Study in Western Germany", in
Boyd C. Shafer et al., *Historical Study in the West*, p. 126.

[2] Georg G. Iggers, *Deutsche Geschichtswissenschaft*, p. 353. (This work
is a revised and extended version of his *The German Conception of
History*.)

[3] Ibid., p. 8. The most eminent of these would have been Franz
Schnabel (1887–1966).

he no longer regards the state in Lutheran-Hegelian-Rankean terms, i.e. as an instrument of Almighty God which is not required to apply the norms of morality in the pursuit of its divine mission. This clear repudiation by Fischer of the statist tradition was actually enunciated as early as 1949 at the first post-war Historians' Conference in Germany at Munich — a courageous act which must have immediately isolated him from the greater body of his colleagues. When one considers the date of his address, it can be regarded as nothing less than an admonition to the Historians' Guild as well as to the Lutheran Church to abandon the traditional view of the state as a God-given force (*gottgegebene Macht*) and also the concomitant Lutheran idea of the "freedom of the Christian man", a doctrine which in secular life meant unquestioning obedience to the state. It was these concepts which had helped to mould the German attitude towards the state. The other possibility would have been, as Fischer then observed, the image of the state as projected in the writings of Imanuel Kant, but this had never been accepted in German thought.[4] The implication that this was disastrous for Germany was made very clear by Fischer at that time. He concluded his excursus with the appeal to German Lutheran Protestantism to develop a "Christian natural law", because only this would enable it to exploit its independence from the state and set about co-operating with both reformed Anglo-Saxon Christianity and the Roman Church, as well as non-Christian humanism in the preservation of the world.[5]

The significance of all this for German historiography can scarcely be overestimated. It was a virtual intellectual revolution which aimed at the re-establishment of normative values as opposed to the essentially national values of German idealism. It was this willingness by Fischer to criticise the *Weltanschauung* of the German intellectual élite prior to 1914 which enabled him to present his explanation of Imperial German policy. Without taking cognizance of this intellectual-historical aspect the resultant explanation would have been but a torso. In short,

[4] Fritz Fischer, "Der deutsche Protestantismus und die Politik im 19. Jahrhundert", *HZ* CLXXXI, p. 476.   [5] Ibid., p. 518.

the fullness of Fischer's account must be attributed to his intellectual-spiritual "conversion" which was signified by his address to the 1949 Historians' Conference in Munich.[6]

What Fischer has shown to have been essential in giving the fullest explanation to date of Imperial German policy has, of course, a universal application. All researchers of national history, whatever the country, must be prepared to investigate the *Gedankenwelt* (world of ideas) and spiritual values of the protagonists in the historical drama, in short, the "unspoken assumptions" to which James Joll has referred.[7] The historian must become acquainted with the "ideological furniture" of the people and societies which he is investigating.[8] It is clear that the methodological problems associated with this would be formidable but there can be no shrinking the responsibility of attempting to unravel the *Weltanschauung* of men in past epochs if something approaching a full historical explanation is to be given for their actions.

Fritz Fischer and his school have made the point very strongly that the prevailing world-view in Imperial Germany was a factor of vast proportions in determining Germany's political stance both domestically and internationally. It is therefore the inescapable duty of the historian to explore this third dimension in his research whatever the country may be. The combination of diplomatic-political, social-economic AND intellectual-spiritual factors, all of which are interrelated, enabled Fritz Fischer to prepare his indictment of Wilhelmine Germany and, by implication, the Third Reich, which tried to impose a grotesque caricature of the "German idea" upon reluctant Europe. Fischer's work is an eloquent declaration that the historian's highest loyalty should not lie in an irrational

[6] It is not coincidental that Wolfgang J. Mommsen describes Fischer's historiography as moralistic or *gesinnungsethisch*. (See his "Domestic Factors . . . ", p. 8). Again, Mommsen refers to the "missionary element" in Fischer's historiography in "Die deutsche 'Weltpolitik' . . . ", p. 484. It is of course completely irrelevant to criticise an historical work for revealing a militant ideological component. Historiography by definition implies ideology.

[7] c.f. James Joll, *The Unspoken Assumptions*, passim.   [8] Ibid., p. 17.

dedication to patriotic sentiment but rather to humanity as a whole, a lesson which could be profitably taken to heart by many writers and teachers of history today, not all of whom by any means live in West Germany.

The Concrete Historiographical Consequences:

It is always a premature exercise to try to assess the long term effects of any revolution just after it has taken place. In any case, however, there are a series of "historiographical consequences" as Imanuel Geiss has noted,[9] which can already be listed as a direct result of the Fischer revolution. It will be profitable to include them here by way of summing up.

(1) The formerly established "orthodox" German thesis of innocence for the outbreak of the First World War is totally destroyed; neither can there be any withdrawal to the "Lloyd George position", namely that the powers slipped into the war, all equally sharing the responsibility. The fact that Germany bore the chief responsibility is no longer disputed, neither can the offensive nature of Germany's policy and war aims be denied. No serious German historian today can venture to pit himself against the evidence compiled by the Fischer school.

(2) As a result, historians of the First World War in all countries now have a completely new basis from which to carry out future research. Indeed, Fischer has stimulated a series of new studies, either directly or indirectly, which will throw fresh light on hitherto unexplored aspects of Wilhelmine and post-Wilhelmine Germany. But beyond this non-German scholars have been inspired to apply Fischer's questions to the history of their own countries and so the "Fischer controversy" has proved doubly fruitful.[10]

(3) For the historical discipline, Fischer's work is an important example of how an apparently closed topic can be profitably reopened by the discovery of hitherto unknown material and by the new questioning of the past that must come

[9] Imanuel Geiss, *Studien über Geschichte und Geschichtswissenschaft,* p. 188.   [10] Ibid., p. 189.

with the passage of time. Indeed, it has shown that the fresh experience of each generation brings with it the need to re-examine the past in the light of that experience. Only with this approach is real progress in the historical discipline possible.

(4) Perhaps at this stage the most productive aspect of the entire controversy has been the fearless assertion of the "continuity" thesis, i.e. the establishing of parallels between German policy first under the Kaiser and then under the Führer, a thesis which will occupy researchers for some time to come.

(5) A further significant aspect of the controversy has been the manner in which the traditional German historians' guild (i.e. the established history professors) have severely discredited themselves. By their often irrational and sometimes even hysterical attacks on Fischer they have shown that they did not dispose over the renowned Rankean objectivity to which they proudly asserted they were committed. To a not inconsiderable extent they have revealed themselves as incorrigible nationalists who uncritically accepted and taught patriotically one-sided versions of their country's past with a virtually religious dogmatism.

(6) Fischer's exposure of the obvious scholarly inadequacies of the traditional guild's approach to national history has unleashed what Professor Hans Herzfeld had termed "the revolt of the younger generation of German historians".[11] Because Fischer has revealed the intolerance and irrationality of the traditionalists, the younger generation of their students are naturally unwilling to accept uncritically (as was the case in the past) the conservative orthodox interpretations which were handed down from the rostrums of West Germany's lecture rooms. The once patriarchal character of the German professor is a thing of the past. Fischer has become the nucleus for a new generation of critical young scholars who were becoming increasingly uneasy in the intellectually sterile and narrow atmosphere of the old guild. Also, older members have been willing to modify their former positions and have moved

[11] Ibid., p. 191.

in some instances very close to that of Fischer, a fact which illustrates that academic magnanimity is not entirely dead in Germany.

The Political Consequences:

As stated in the introduction, there is a reciprocal effect between historiography and politics. This is illustrated supremely well in the modern German experience. Historiography generally has always been one of the most important means of perpetuating an ideology, and the "ruling classes" have employed it to their own advantage with great success. On the other hand a critical historiography has the effect of liberating people from the intellectual imprisonment of that ideology. This has taken place dramatically in Germany by the ruthless sweeping away of the traditional propaganda regarding Germany's role in the First World War. There have been a series of important political consequences.

The orthodox apologia was in the form of a chain of arguments which began with the "Encirclement" myth followed by the alleged attack on Germany in 1914, then Versailles, reparations and inflation leading to the word economic crisis, to Hitler and the Third Reich. The aim was to explain National Socialism, the German version of Fascism, as having nothing to do with the main stream of German history, and also to show that Germany was not totally responsible for the Second World War.

For the citizen of the Federal Republic (which regards itself as the successor to the German Reich) who now sees that there was no Encirclement before 1914, and that the Great War was not a war of national defence but rather one of aggression and conquest, will no longer be able to point to Versailles, the reparations and the depression as the excuse for the rise of Nazism. He will have to admit, too, that the Second World War was essentially a German war of *revanche* for the defeat in the 1914–18 war with strikingly similar war aims. Further, such a newly enlightened citizen will also have to admit that

Germany having begun the war and lost it (1945), would morally have to pay some price, not only to the West but to the East. In this situation the price consists in accepting among other things the Oder-Neisse Line and in living in a sensible and peaceful relationship with the Eastern European states. And, further, if such a citizen really wishes to draw lessons from his country's recent history (so Imanuel Geiss), he must recognise that Germany may not exercise power to the degree which would enable her to assume that hegemonial position in Central Europe which she strove to achieve twice previously in this century and which for short periods, she actually attained.

In the present situation as developed since 1945, Germany is of necessity required to accept the status of a middle power in Europe, to accept the logic of coming to an arrangement with the German Democratic Republic as the final proof of liquidation of all those dreams of empire which drove Germany to war with the world twice in this century. Any attempt by West Germany to avoid recognising these consequences would have to lead to a third phase of German power politics, the results of which would be catastrophic.

A critical observer of West Germany's social and political growth since the war could not imagine the above consequences being spelled out so ruthlessly in public ten years ago. To do so would have been considered heretical and the writer or speaker branded as a traitor. The radically improved intellectual-political climate in Germany in which the hysteria over reunification has dramatically subsided to enable a new *Ostpolitik,* is intimately bound up with the change in the historical consciousness brought about to a large extent by the Fischer controversy. Conservatives with their inborn affinity for political power have quickly recognised the above consequences. It is now impossible for a Franz Josef Strauss to stir up any effective emotional response among his countrymen trying to convince them that Germany has been unjustly treated by the allies of the Second World War. The present bitterness among conservatives, both in scholarship as in politics, is only explicable in terms of their frustration. The new research of the Fischer school has robbed them of their most emotively convincing arguments by illustrating that they are no longer morally tenable.

To underline what was stated at the beginning, the fact that Fischer and his school now "survive" is eloquent commentary on the state of democracy in West Germany. In the Weimar Republic scholars who ventured to oppose the orthodox apologia re "Encirclement" and the "War Guilt" were victimised and denied academic posts. In the Third Reich such scholars were effectively silenced. Immediately after 1945 the publication of critical works of scholarship about the origins and course of the First World War simply did not occur. Only in the early 'sixties was that possible; a basic revision of German history in the Great War was finally seen necessary as a task of liberating the country from the incubus of a political taboo. The men with the courage to embark on this task have, as has been noted, had to endure years of bitter controversy. Thus they have withstood all the severe attacks and now a great moral victory has been won. The entire controversy and its outcome has been both a reflection and a cause of the ever deepening democratisation of West German society, a process which can scarcely be reversed by normal political means.[12]

[12] Ibid., p. 197. For an illustration of the importance of the "historical perspective" in politics see Lawrence L. Whetton, *Germany's Ostpolitik*, pp. 93–114. Whetton correctly observes that the West German critics of *Ostpolitik* were those who "adhered to the history of the Bismarckian model for German unity, based on a unitarian *kleindeutsche Lösung* (solution) formula (drawing strength largely from the conservative segment of the electorate). Supporters for the latter position gravitated towards the CDU, which campaigned on a neo-Bismarckian platform" (p. 106). The more that historical research is able to expose the internal defects of Bismarckian Germany as well as its ruthless disregard for the principle of national self-determination, especially towards the Poles, the more the moral claim for the restoration of the Reich to its 1939 borders becomes illusory. The Fischer school has done more than any other scholarly group in West Germany to explode any historically based moral claims for reunification. The endorsement of Brandt's *Ostpolitik* represents a change in the historical-political consciousness of West Germans, a change which would have been impossible had not historians successfully "de-bunked" the Bismarckian-Wilhelmine image of the Reich.

BIBLIOGRAPHY

There are two reasons for appending a select bibliography to this essay. First, there was the need to list the works consulted in its preparation, and second, it was thought desirable to provide students with the titles of books and articles which constitute the material most centrally relevant to this subject. No attempt has been made to include those well-known but now superseded works on the origins of the First World War. If the list has any special merit, it lies in the fact that it has included those monographs and articles which reflect the present intellectual ferment in German academic circles. Titles which the reader may miss here could be found in the present writer's *The War Aims of Imperial Germany: Professor Fritz Fischer and His Critics* (Brisbane, 1968).

ACTON, J. E. E. D., Lord, "German Schools of History", *EHR* I (1886), pp. 7–42.

ASENDORF, MANFRED, *Aus der Aufklärung in die permanente Restauration-Geschichtswissenschaft in Deutschland* (Hamburg, 1974).

BAILYN, BERNARD, *The Ideological Origins of the American Revolution* (Cambridge, Mass., 1967).

BARKIN, KENNETH D., *The Controversy over German Industrialisation 1890–1902* (Chicago/London, 1970).

———, "Conflict and Concord in Wilhelmian Social Thought", *CEH* V (1972), pp. 55–71.

BAUMGART, WINFRIED, *Deutschland im Zeitalter des Imperialismus* (Frankfurt am Main, 1972).

BECKER, CARL, What is Historiography?, *AHR* XLIVC (1938), pp. 20–28.

BEHM, ERIKA, and KUCZYNSKI, JÜRGEN, "Arthur Dix: Propagandist der wirtschaftlichen Vorbereitung des ersten Weltkrieges", *JWG* 11 (1970), pp. 69–100.

BERGHAHN, VOLKER R., "Zu den Zielen des deutschen Flottenbaus unter Wilhelm II.", *HZ* CCX (1970), pp. 34–100.

———, *Der Tirpitz-Plan. Genesis und Verfall einer innenpolitischen Krisenstrategie unter Wilhelm II.* (Düsseldorf, 1971).

———, "Das Kaiserreich in der Sackgasse", *NPL* XVI (1971), pp. 494–506.

————, *Rüstung und Machtpolitik* (Düsseldorf, 1973).

————, *Germany and the Approach of War in 1914* (London, 1973).

————, "Fritz Fischer und seine Schüler", *NPL* 11 (1974), pp. 143–154.

BERTHOLD, WERNER, *Grosshungern und Gehorchen. Zur Entstehung und politischen Funktion der Geschichtsideologie des westdeutschen Imperialismus* (East Berlin, 1960).

BESSON, WALDEMAR, and HILLER VON GAERTRINGEN, FRIEDRICH, FREIHERR (eds.), *Geschichte und Gegenwartsbewusstsein. Festschrift für Hans Rothfels zum 70. Geburtstag* (Göttingen, 1963).

BÖHME, HELMUT, *Deutschlands Weg zur Grossmacht* (Frankfurt, 1966).

BOWEN, RALPH H., *German Theories of the Corporative State* (New York, 1971).

BRANDS, M. C., *Historisme als Ideologie. Het "Anti-Normatieve" en "onpolitieke" Element in de duitse Geschiedwetenschap* (Assen, 1965).

BURCHARDT, LOTHAR, *Friedenswirtschaft und Kriegsvorsorge—Deutschlands wirtschaftliche Rüstungsbestrebungen* (Boppard am Rhein, 1968).

BUTTERFIELD, HERBERT, *Man on His Past* (Cambridge, 1969).

CARLSON, ANDREW R., *German Foreign Policy, 1890–1914 and Colonial Policy to 1914: a Handbook and Annotated Bibliography* (Metuchen, N.J., 1970).

CARSTEN, FRANCIS L., "Living with the Past. What German Historians are Saying", *Encounter,* no. 127 (April 1964), pp. 106–110.

————, Review of *Deutschland in der Weltpolitik des 19. and 20. Jahrhunderts,* edited by I. Geiss and B. J. Wendt, *MGM* XV (1974), pp. 232–235.

CONZE, WERNER, *Die Deutsche Nation. Ergebnis der Geschichte* (Göttingen, 1965).

DAHLIN, EBBA, *French and German Public Opinion on Declared War Aims 1914–1918* (London: Stanford University Press, 1930).

Das Argument 70. Kritik der bürgerlichen Geschichtswissenschaft (1), Sonderband der Zeitschrift für Philosophie und Sozialwissenschaften (Berlin, 1972).

Das Argument 75. Kritik der bürgerlichen Geschichtswissenschaft (11), Sonderband der Zeitschrift für Philosophie und Sozialwissenschaften (Berlin, 1972).

DEHIO, LUDWIG, *Germany and World Politics in the Twentieth Century* (London, 1960).

DELBRÜCK, HANS, *Government and the Will of the People* (New York, 1923).

DESCHNER, KARLHEINZ, ed., *Wer lehrt an deutschen Universitäten?* (Wiesbaden, 1968).

DEWEY, JOHN, *German Philosophy and Politics* (1915; reprint, New York, 1970).

DORPALEN, ANDREAS, "Historiography as History: The Work of Gerhard Ritter", *JMH* XXXIV (1962), pp. 1–18.

DÜDING, DIETER, *Der Nationalsoziale Verein 1896–1903* (Munich, Vienna, 1972).

ELEY, GEOFF, "Sammlungspolitik, Social Imperialism and the Navy Law of 1898", *MGM* XV (1974), pp. 29–63.

EPSTEIN, KLAUS, "Gerhard Ritter and the First World War", *JCH* I, no. 3 (1966), pp. 193–210.

ENGEL-JANOSI, FRIEDRICH, *Die Wahrheit der Geschichte. Versuche zur Geschichtsschreibung in der Neuzeit* (Munich, 1973).

ERDMANN, KARL DIETRICH, "Zur Beurteilung Bethmann Hollwegs", *GWU* XV (1964), pp. 525–540.

EYCK, ERICH, *Das persönliche Regiment Wilhelm II. Politische Geschichte des deutschen Kaiserreiches von 1890 bis 1914* (Erlenback-Zurich, 1948).

FABER, KARL GEORG, *Theorie der Geschichtswissenschaft* (Munich, 1972).

FARRAR, LANCELOT L., *The Short-War Illusion—German Policy, Strategy and Domestic Affairs, August–December 1914* (Santa Barbara and Oxford, 1973).

FAULENBACH, BERND, ed., *Geschichtswissenschaft in Deutschland* (Munich, 1974).

FELDMAN, GERALD D., ed., *German Imperialism 1914–1918: The Development of a Historical Debate* (New York, 1972).

FERRO, MARC, *The Great War 1914–1918* (London, 1973).

FISCHER, FRITZ, "Der Deutsche Protestantismus und die Politik im 19. Jahrhundert", *HZ* CLXXXI (1951), pp. 473–518.

————, *Griff nach der Weltmacht. Die Kriegszielpolitik des kaiserlichen Deutschlands 1914/1918* (Düsseldorf, 1961).

————, *Germany's Aims in the First World War* (London, 1967). (English translation of the previous title).

————, *Krieg der Illusionen Die deutsche Politik von 1911 bis 1914,* (Düsseldorf, 1969).

————, *War of Illusions* (London, 1974). (English translation of the previous title).

————, "Aufgaben und Methoden der Geschichtswissenschaft" in *Geschichtsschreibung—Epochen, Methoden, Gestaltung,* edited by Jürgen Scheskewitz (Düsseldorf, 1971), pp. 7–28.

————, *World Power or Decline—The controversy over Germany's Aims in the First World War* (New York, 1974).

FRANKE, BRUNO WILHELM, "Handelsneid und Grosse Politik in den deutsch–englischen Beziehungen 1871-1914", *ZP* XXIX (1939), pp. 455–475.

FRICKE, DIETER, "Der deutsche Imperialismus und die Reichstagwahlen von 1907", *ZfG,* (1961), pp. 538–576.

FULLER, LEON W., The War of 1914 as Interpreted by German Intellectuals", *JMH* XIV (1942), pp. 145–160.

GASSER, ADOLF, "Deutschlands Entschluss zum Präventivkrieg 1913/14", in *Discordia Concors. Festgabe für Edgar Bonjour zu seinem 70. Geburtstag* (Basel/Stuttgart, 1968), pp. 173–224.

——, "Der deutsche Hegemonialkrieg von 1914" in *Deutschland in der Weltpolitik des 19. und 20. Jahrhundert*, edited by I. Geiss and B. J. Wendt (Düsseldorf, 1973), pp. 307–340.

——, "Erster Weltkrieg und 'Friedensforschung' ", *ASMZ* Mai (1974), pp. 235–238.

GEISS, IMANUEL, and POGGE VON STRANDMANN, HARTMUT, *Die Erforderlichkeit des Unmöglichen* (Frankfurt am Main, 1965).

GEISS, IMANUEL, "Franz Josef Strauss—'Retter des Vaterlands' ", *WH*, 25 (Oktober, 1971), pp. 291–309.

——, *Die Rechtsopposition und ihr Kampf gegen die Ostverträge*, no. 9, Schriftenreihe des "Pressediensts der Demokratischen Aktion" (Munich, 1972).

——, Weltherrschaft durch Hegemonie—Die deutsche Politik im 1. Weltkrieg nach den Riezler Tagebüchern", *APZ* B50 (9 December 1972), pp. 3–22.

——, *Studien zur Geschichte und Geschichtswissenschaft* (Frankfurt am Main, 1972).

——, "Kurt Riezler und der erste Weltkrieg" in *Deutschland in der Weltpolitik des 19. und 20. Jahrhunderts*, edited by I. Geiss and B. J. Wendt (Düsseldorf, 1973), pp. 398–418.

——, "Reich und Nation", *APZ* B15 (14 April 1973), pp. 3–25.

——, *Was wird aus der Bundesrepublik—Die Deutschen zwischen Sozialismus und Revolution* (Hamburg, 1973).

——, "Die Westdeutsche Geschichtsschreibung seit 1945", *JIDG* III (1974), pp. 417–455.

——, "The German Empire and Imperialism 1871–1914", *AJPH* XX (1974), pp. 11–21.

——, and TAMCHINA, RAINER, *Ansichten einer künftigen Geschichtswissenschaft* 2 vols. (Munich, 1974).

GRENVILLE, J. A. S., "Lansdowne's Abortive Project of 12 March 1901 for a Secret Agreement with Germany, *BIHR* XXVII (1954), pp. 281–213.

GROH, DIETER, " 'Je eher desto besser!' Innenpolitische Faktoren für die Präventivkriegsbereitschaft des deutschen Reiches 1913/14", *PVS* XIII (1972), pp. 501–521.

——, "Strukturgeschichte als 'totale' Geschichte", *VSSWG* LVIII (1971), pp. 288–322.

——, "Die misslungene 'innere Reichsgründung'. Verfassung, Wirtschaft und Sozialpolitik im zweiten Reiche", *R d'A* IV (1972), pp. 89–112.

———, *Negative Integration und revolutionäre Attentismus. Die deutsche Sozialdemokratie am Vorabend des ersten Weltkrieges* (Frankfurt am Main and Berlin, 1973).

GORDON, MICHAEL R., "Domestic Conflict and the Origins of the First World War: The British and German Cases", *JMH* XLVI (1974), pp. 191–226.

GÖRLITZ, WALTER, ed. *Der Kaiser . . .* Aufzeichnungen des Chefs des Marinekabinetts Admiral Alexander von Müller über die Ära Wilhelms II (Göttingen, 1965).

GUILLAND, ANTOINE, *Modern Germany and Her Historians* (London, 1915; reprint, Westport, Conn., 1970).

GURATZSCH, DANKWART, *Macht durch Organisation—Die Grundlegung des Hugenbergschen Presseimperiums* (Düsseldorf, 1974).

HALLGARTEN, G. W. F., *Imperialismus vor 1914*, 2nd revised ed., 2 vols. (Munich, 1963).

———, *Das Schicksal des Imperialismus im 20. Jahrhundert* (Frankfurt am Main, 1969).

———, *Als die Schatten fielen* (Frankfurt am Main, 1969).

HATTON, P. H. S., "Harcourt and Solf: The Search for an Anglo-German Understanding through Africa, 1912–1914", *ESR* 1 (1971), pp. 123–145.

———, "The Debate on the July Crisis Continues: Professor Fischer's second volume and its aftermath", *ESR* IV (1974), pp. 165–173.

HEIBER, HELMUT, *Walter Frank und sein Reichsinstitut für Geschichte des neuen Deutschlands* (Stuttgart, 1966).

HERZFELD, HANS, "Germany: after the Catastrophe", *JCH* II (1967), pp. 79–92.

HILDEBRAND, KLAUS, *Bethmann Hollweg. Der Kanzler ohne Eigenschaften* (Düsseldorf, 1970).

HILLGRUBER, ANDREAS, "Riezlers Theorie des kalkulierten Risikos und Bethmann Hollwegs politische Konzeption in der Julikrise 1914", *HZ* CCII (1966), pp. 331–351.

———, *Deutschlands Rolle in der Vorgeschichte der beiden Weltkriege* (Göttingen, 1967).

———, *Kontinuität und Diskontinuität in der deutschen Aussenpolitik von Bismarck bis Hitler* (Düsseldorf, 1969).

HINSLEY, F. H., *The Causes of the First World War* (Hull, 1964).

HIRSCH, HELMUT, *Lehrer machen Geschichte* (Wuppertal, 1971).

HÖHN, REINHARD, *Sozialismus und Heer: Der Kampf des Heeres gegen die Sozialdemokratie*, 3 vols. (Bad Harzburg, 1969).

HOLBRAAD, CARSTEN, *The Concert of Europe—A Study in German and British International Theory 1815—1914* (London, 1970).

HOLLINGER, DAVID A., "T. S. Kuhn's Theory of Science and its Implications for History", *AHR* LXXVIII (1973), pp. 370–393.

HOLSTI, OLE R., NORTH, ROBERT C., and BRODY, RICHARD A., "Percep-
tion and Action in the 1914 Crisis" in *Quantitative International
Politics: Insights and Evidence,* edited by David J. Singer (New
York, 1968), pp. 123–158.

HÖLZLE, ERWIN, "Griff nach der Weltmacht?", *HPB* X (1962), pp. 65–69.

———, *Der Geheimverrat und der Kriegsausbruch 1914* (Göttingen,
1973).

HUBATSCH, WALTHER, *Die Ära Tirpitz. Studien zur deutschen Marinepolitik 1890–1918* (Göttingen, 1955).

IGGERS, GEORG G., *The German Conception of History* (Middletown,
Conn., 1968).

———, *Die deutsche Geschichtswissenschaft,* 2nd ed. (Munich, 1972).

JANIS, IRVING L., *Victims of Groupthink; a psychological study of
foreign policy decisions and fiascos* (Boston, 1972).

JANNSEN, KARL-HEINZ, *Der Kanzler und der General: Die Führungskrise
um Bethmann Hollweg und Falkenhayn 1914–1916* (Göttingen,
1967).

JARAUSCH, KONRAD K., "The Illusion of Limited War: Chancellor
Bethmann Hollweg's Calculated Risk, July 1914", *CEH* II (1969),
pp. 48–76.

———, "World Power or Tragic Fate? The *Kriegsschuldfrage* as
Historical Neurosis", *CEH* V (1972), pp. 72–92.

———, *The Enigmatic Chancellor. Bethmann Hollweg and the Hubris
of Imperial Germany* (New Haven and London, 1973).

———, "Die Alldeutschen und die Regierung Bethmann Hollweg—Eine
Denkschrift Kurt Riezlers vom Herbst 1916", *VZ* XXI (1973),
pp. 435–468.

JERUSSALIMSKI, A. S., *Der deutsche Imperialismus. Geschichte und
Gegenwart* (East Berlin, 1968).

JOLL, JAMES, *1914: The Unspoken Assumptions* (London, 1968).

KAELBLE, HARTMUT, *Industrielle Interessenpolitik in der wilhelminischen
Gesellschaft—Centralverband Deutscher Industrieller 1895–1914*
(Berlin, 1967).

KANTOROWICZ, HERMANN, *The Spirit of British Policy and the Myth of
the Encirclement of Germany* (London, 1931).

———, *Gutachen zur Kriegsschuldfrage 1914,* edited by Imanuel Geiss
(Frankfurt am Main, 1967).

KEHR, ECKART, *Schlachtflottenbau und Parteipolitik 1894–1901* (Berlin,
1930; reprint: 1965).

———, *Der Primat der Innenpolitik* (Berlin, 1965).

KENNEDY, PAUL M., "Tirpitz, England and the Second Navy Law of 1900:
A Strategical Critique", *MGM* II (1970), pp. 33–57.

———, "The Decline of Nationalistic History in the West, 1900–1970",
JCH VIII (1973), pp. 77–100.

KIELMANNSEGG, PETER GRAF, *Deutschland und der Erste Weltkrieg* (Frankfurt am Main, 1968).

KITZMÜLLER, ERICH; KUBY, HEINZ; and NIETHAMMER, LUTZ, "Der Wandel der nationalen Frage in der Bundesrepublik Deutschland", *APZ*, vol 33 (18 August 1973), pp. 3–30, and vol. 34 (25 August 1973), pp. 3–30.

KJELLEN, RUDOLF, *Die Grossmächte der Gegenwart* (Leipzig and Berlin, 1918).

KLEIN, FRITZ, *Deutschland 1897/98–1917. Deutschland in der Periode des Imperialismus bis zur Grossen Sozialistischen Oktoberrevolution* (East Berlin, 1969).

———, (General Editor), *Deutschland im Ersten Weltkrieg* 3 vols., (East Berlin, 1969).

KOCH, H. W., "The Anglo-German Alliance Negotiations: Missed Opportunity or Myth?, *History* LIV (1969), pp. 378–392.

———, *The Origins of the First World War. Great Power Rivalry and German War Aims* (London, 1973).

KOEHL, ROBERT, "A Prelude to Hitler's Greater Germany", *AHR* (1953), pp. 43–65.

KÖHLER, ERNST, *Bildungsbürgertum und nationale Politik. Eine Studie zum politischen Denken Otto Hintzes* (Bad Homburg, 1970).

KOHN, HANS, ed., *German History—Some New German Views* (London, 1954).

KOLLMAN, ERIC C., "Wather Rathenau and German Foreign Policy— Thoughts and Action", *JMH* XXIV (1952), pp. 127–142.

KRILL, HANS-HEINZ, *Die Ranke-Renaissance—Max Lenz und Erich Marcks* (Berlin, 1962).

KUHN, THOMAS S., *The Structure of Scientific Revolutions* (Chicago, 1970).

KÜHNL, REINHARD, *Geschichte als Ideologie, Kritische Analyse bundesdeutscher Geschichtsbücher* (Hamburg 1973).

LABUDA, GERARD, "The Slavs in Nineteenth Century German Historiography", *PWA* (1969), pp. 177–234.

LAQUER, WALTER, and MOSSE, GEORGE L., eds., *The New History— Trends in Historical Research and Writing since World War II* (New York, 1967).

LAUE, THEODOR VON, *Leopold Ranke—The Formative Years* (Princeton, 1950).

LEFF, GORDON, *History and Social Theory* (London, 1969).

LERNER, MAX, *Ideas are Weapons—The History and Uses of Ideas* (New York, 1940).

LOSEK, GERHARD; MEIER, HELMUT; and SCHMIDT, WALTER, eds., *Unbewältigte Vergangenheit. Handbuch zur Auseinandersetzung mit der westdeutschen bürgerlichen Geschichtsschreibung* (East Berlin, 1971).

LOWE, C. J. and DOCKRILL, M. L., *The Mirage of Power. British Foreign Policy 1902–14*, 3 vols. (London and Boston, 1972).

LUDWIG, EMIL, *Wilhelm der Zweite* (Frankfurt/Main and Hamburg, 1968) (Fischer Bücherei edition with an epilogue by Imanuel Geiss).

MAEHL, WILLIAM H., "Germany's War Aims in the East, 1914–17: Status of the Question", *TH* XXIV (1972), pp. 381–406.

MARCZEWSKI, JERZY, "German Historiography and the Problem of Germany's Responsibility for World War I", *PWA* XII (1971), pp. 289–308.

MAY, ERNEST R., *"Lessons" of the Past—The Use and Misuse of History in American Foreign Policy* (New York, 1973).

MENDE, DIETRICH, "Die nicht bewältigte Vergangenheit des Ersten Weltkrieges", *EA* IX (1963), pp. 333–354.

MCCLELLAND, CHARLES E., *The German Historians and England: A Study in Nineteenth Century Views* (Cambridge, 1971).

MOMMSEN, HANS, "Historical Scholarship in Transition: The Situation in the Federal Republic of Germany", *Daedalus* 100 (1971), pp. 485–508.

MOMMSEN, WOLFGANG J., "The Debate on German War Aims, *JCH* I, no. 3 (1966), pp. 47–72.

————, *Die Geschichtswissenschaft jenseits des Historismus* (Düsseldorf, 1970).

————, "Zur Kriegsschuldfrage 1914", *HZ* CCXII (1971), pp. 606–614.

————, "Die Deutsche 'Weltpolitik' und der Erste Weltkrieg", *NPL* XVI (1971), pp. 482–493.

————, "Domestic Factors in German Foreign Policy before 1914", *CEH* VI (1973), pp. 3–43.

————, "Die latente Krise des Wilhelminischen Reiches: Staat und Gesellschaft in Deutschland 1890–1914", *MGM* XV (1974), pp. 7–28.

MOSES, JOHN A., *The War Aims of Imperial Germany: Professor Fritz Fischer and his Critics* (Brisbane, 1968).

————, "The Crisis in West German Historiography: Origins and Trends", *HS* XIII (1969), pp. 445–459.

————, "Pan Germanism and the German Professors 1914–1918", *AJPH* XV (1969), pp. 45–60.

————, Review Article of *Krieg der Illusionen* by Fritz Fischer, *AJPH* XVI (1970), pp. 436–441.

————, "The July Crisis 1914: Historiography and Weltanschauung" in *Questioning the Past*, edited by D. P. Crook (Brisbane, 1972), pp. 322–335.

————, "Karl Dietrich Erdmann, The Riezler Diary and the Fischer Controversy", *JES* III (1973), pp. 241–254.

————, "Hitler between Prussianism and Mass Hysteria—Some Post-War German Views", *UNHJ* III (1975), pp. 27–43.

MÜLLER, KARL ALEXANDER VON, *Mars und Venus—Erinnerungen 1914–1918* (Stuttgart, 1954).

NITSCHKE, AUGUST, "German Politics and Medieval History, *JCH* III, no. 2 (1968), pp. 75–92.

NOLTE, ERNST, "Uber das Verhältnis von bürgerlicher und 'marxistischer' Geschichtswissenschaft", *APZ*, vol. 31 (4 August 1973), pp. 10–21.

OHNO, EIJI, "German Economic Policy in Transition—The Policy of Uniting versus Radical Union", *KUER* (1965), pp. 20–41.

POIS, ROBERT A., *Friedrich Meinecke and German Politics* (Berkeley, 1972).

PROSS, HARRY, ed., *Die Zerstörung der deutschen Politik. Dokumente 1871–1933* (Frankfurt am Main, 1959).

PUHLE, HANS-JÜRGEN, *Agrarische Interessenpolitik und preussischer Konservatismus im Wilhelminischen Reich (1893–1914)* (Hannover, 1966),

RANKE, LEOPOLD VON, *Die Grossen Mächte—Politisches Gespräch* (Göttingen, 1958).

———, *The Theory and Practice of History*, edited with an introduction by Georg G. Iggers and Konrad von Moltke (New York, 1973).

RANTZAU, JOHANN ALBRECHT VON, "The Glorification of the State in German Historical Writing" in *German History: Some New German Views*, edited by Hans Kohn (London, 1954), pp. 157–174.

Reichsgründung, 1870/71 (Stuttgart, 1970).

RADKAU, JOACHIM, "Geschichtswissenschaft heute—Ende der Selbstmystifikation?", *NPL*, Part 1, XVII (1972), pp. 1–41; Part II, XVII (1972), pp. 141–166.

RADKAU, JOACHIM and ORLINDE, *Praxis der Geschichtswissenschaft. Die Desorientiertheit des historischen Interesses* (Düsseldorf, 1972).

RATHENAU, WALTER, *Tagebuch 1907–1922*, edited and commented by Hartmut Pogge von Strandmann with a contribution by James Joll and an introduction by Fritz Fischer (Düsseldorf, 1967).

REIN, G. A., *Sir John Robert Seeley—Eine Studie über den Historiker* (Langensalza, 1912).

REMAK, JOACHIM, "1914—The Third Balkan War: Origins Reconsidered", *JMH* XLIII (1971), pp. 353–366.

RIEZLER, KURT, *Die Erforderlichkeit des Unmöglichen* (Munich, 1913).

———, (J. J. Ruedorffer) *Gründzuge der Weltpolitik in der Gegenwart* (Stuttgart and Berlin), 1914).

———, *Tagebücher, Aufsätze, Dokumente*, edited with introduction by Karl Dietrich Erdmann (Göttingen, 1967).

RINGER, FRITZ, *The Decline of the German Mandarins* (Cambridge, Mass., 1969).

RITTER, GERHARD, *Die Legende von der verschmähten englischen Freundschaft 1898–1901* (Freiburg, 1929).

———, *Geschichte als Bildungsmacht* (Stuttgart, 1947).

RITTER, GERHARD, *Staatskunst und Kriegshandwerk. Das Problem des Militarismus in Deutschland*, 4 vols. (Munich, 1964–65).

———, *Der Erste Weltkrieg. Studien zum deutschen Geschichtsbild* (Bonn, 1964).

———, *The German Problem* (Chicago, 1965).

RÖHL, J. C. G., "The Disintegration of the Kartell and the Politics of Bismarck's Fall from Power, 1887–90, *HJ* IX (1966), pp. 60–69.

———, "Admiral von Müller and the Approach of War, 1911–1914", *HJ* XII (1969), pp. 651–673.

———, *From Bismarck to Hitler* (London, 1970).

———, *Zwei deutsche Fürsten zur Kriegsschuldfrage: Lichnowsky und Eulenburg und der Ausbruch des ersten Weltkrieges* (Düsseldorf, (1971).

———, *1914: Delusion or Design? The Testimony of Two German Diplomats* (London, 1973). (English translation of the previous title.)

ROTH, W. et al., *Schwarzbuch: Franz Josef Strauss* (Cologne, 1972).

ROTHWELL, V. H., *British War Aims and Peace Diplomacy 1914–1918* (Oxford, 1971).

SCHAFF, ADAM, *Geschichte und Wahrheit* (Vienna, 1970).

SCHENK, WILLY, *Die deutsch-englische Rivalität vor dem ersten Weltkrieg in der Sicht deutscher Historiker* (Aarau, 1967).

SCHESKEWITZ, JÜRGEN, ed., *Geschichtsschreibung—Epochen, Methoden, Gestaltung* (Düsseldorf, 1971).

SCHIEDER, THEODOR, *Geschichte als Wissenschaft* (Munich and Vienna, 1965).

SCHIEDER, WOLFGANG, ed., *Erster Weltkrieg: Ursachen, Entstehung und Kriegsziele* (Cologne and Berlin, 1969).

SCHLENKE, MANFRED, "Das 'preussische Beispiel' in Propaganda und Politik des Nationalsozialismus", *APZ*, B27 (3 July 1968), pp. 15–23.

SCHMIDT, GUSTAV, *Deutscher Historismus und der Übergang zur parlamentarischen Demokratie* (Lübeck and Hamburg, 1964).

———, "Innenpolitische Blockbildungen in Deutschland am Vorabend des Ersten Weltkrieges", *APZ*, B20 (1972), pp. 3–32.

SCHOTTELIUS, HERBERT, and DEIST, WILHELM, eds., *Marine und Marinepolitik im Kaiserlichen Deutschland 1871–1914* (Düsseldorf, 1972).

SCHRAEPLER, ERNST, "Die Forschung über den Ausbruch des Ersten Weltkrieges im Wandel des Geschichtsbildes 1919–1969", *GWU* XXIII (1972), pp. 321–338.

SCHROEDER, PAUL W., "World War I as Galloping Gertie: A Reply to Joachim Remak", *JMH* XLIV (1972), pp. 319–345.

SCHWABE, KLAUS, *Wissenschaft und Kriegsmoral. Die deutschen Hochschullehrer und die politischen Grundfragen des Ersten Weltkrieges* (Göttingen, 1969).

SCHAFER, BOYD C., et al., *Historical Study in the West* (New York, 1968).

SIRACUSA, JOSEPH M., *New Left Diplomatic Histories and Historians— The American Revisionists* (Port Washington and London, 1973).

SOMBART, WERNER, *Händler und Helden—Patriotische Besinnung* (Munich and Leipzig, 1915).

SRBIK, HEINRICH RITTER VON, *Geist und Geschichte vom Deutschen Humanismus bis zur Gegenwart*, 2 vols. (2nd ed., Salzburg, 1964).

STEGMANN, DIRK, *Die Erben Bismarks. Sammlungspolitik 1897–1918* (Cologne and Berlin, 1970).

STERLING, RICHARD W., *Ethics in a World Power. The Political Ideas of Friedrich Meinecke* (Princeton, 1958).

STERN, FRITZ, "Bethmann Hollweg and the War: The Limits of Responsibility" in *The Responsibility of Power*, edited by Leonard Krieger and Fritz Stern (London/Melbourne, 1968).

———, *The Failure of Illiberalism—Essays on the Political Culture of Germany* (London, 1972).

STIRK, S. D., *The Prussian Spirit. A Survey of German Literature and Politics 1914–1940* (Port Washington, N.Y., 1969).

STREISAND, JOACHIM, ed., *Die deutsche Geschichtswissenschaft vom Beginn des 19. Jahrhunderts bis zur Reichseinigung von oben* (2nd revised ed., East Berlin, 1969).

———, *Die bürgerliche deutsche Geschichtsschreibung von der Reichseinigung von oben bis zur Befreiung Deutschlands vom Faschismus* (East Berlin, 1965).

STROMBERG, ROLAND N., "The Intellectuals and the Coming of War in 1914", *JES* III (1973), pp. 109–122.

STRAUSS, LEO, "Kurt Riezler", *SR* XIII (1956), pp. 3–34.

STÜRMER, MICHAEL, ed., *Das kaiserliche Deutschland—Politik und Gesellschaft 1870–1918* (Düsseldorf, 1970).

SYWOTTEK, ARNOLD, "Die Fischer-Kontroverse. Ein Beitrag zur Entwicklung historisch-politischen Bewusstseins in der Bundesrepublik" in *Deutschland in der Weltpolitik des 19. and 20. Jahrhunderts*, edited by I. Geiss and B. J. Wendt (Düsseldorf, 1973), pp. 19–48.

TAYLOR, A. J. P., *The Trouble Makers. Dissent over Foreign Policy 1792–1939* (London, 1957).

THIMME, ANNELISE, *Hans Delbrück als Kritiker der Wilhelminischen Epoche* (Düsseldorf, 1955).

TÖPNER, KURT, *Gelehrte Politiker und politisierende Gelehrte* (Göttingen, 1970).

TREITSCHKE, HEINRICH VON, *History of Germany in the Nineteenth Century*, vol. 1 (London, 1915).

TURNER, L. C., *Origins of the First World War* (London, 1970).

VAGTS, ALFRED, "M. M. Warburg & Co. Ein Bankhaus in der deutschen Weltpolitik 1905–1933", *VSSWG* XLV (1958), pp. 289–388.

VIERHAUS, RUDOLF, *Ranke und die Soziale Welt* (Münster, 1957).

VIETSCH, EBERHARD VON, *Wilhelm Solf: Botschafter zwischen den Zeiten* (Tübingen, 1961).

——, *Bethmann Hollweg: Staatsmann zwischen Macht und Ethos* (Boppard am Rhein, 1969).

VOGEL, BARBARA, *Deutsche Russlandpolitik. Das Scheitern der deutschen Weltpolitik unter Bülow 1900–1906* (Düsseldorf, 1973).

VOM BROCKE, BERNHARD, *Kurt Breysig—Geschichtswissenschaft zwischen Historismus und Soziologie* (Lübeck and Hamburg, 1971).

WALLACH, JEHUDA L., *Das Dogma der Vernichtungsschlacht. Die Lehren von Clausewitz und Schlieffen und ihre Wirkungen in zwei Weltkriegen* (Frankfurt am Main, 1967).

WEBER, FRANK G., *Eagles on the Crescent—Germany, Austria and the Diplomacy of the Turkish Alliance 1914–1918* (Ithica and London, 1970).

WEHLER, HANS-ULRICH, ed., *Moderne deutsche soziale Geschichte* (Cologne and Berlin, 1966).

——, *Krisenherde des Kaiserreiches 1871–1918* (Göttingen, 1970).

——, ed., *Deutsche Historiker,* 5 vols. (Göttingen, 1971–72).

——, ed., *Geschichte und Soziologie,* (Cologne, 1972).

——, ed., *Geschichte und Ökonomie* (Cologne, 1973).

——, *Geschichte als historische Sozialwissenshaft* (Frankfurt am Main, 1973).

——, ed., *Sozialgeschichte heute* (Göttingen, 1974).

WERNECKE, KLAUS, *Der Wille zur Weltgeltung: Aussenpolitik und Öffentlichkeit im Kaiserreich am Vorabend des Ersten Weltkrieges* (Düsseldorf, 1970).

WEYMAR, ERNST, *Das Selbstverständnis der Deutschen* (Stuttgart, 1961).

WHETTON, LAWRENCE L., *Germany's Ostpolitik* (Oxford, 1971).

WILLIAMSON, SAMUEL, *The Politics of Grand Strategy—Britain and France Prepare for War, 1904–1914* (Cambridge, Mass., 1969).

WISE, GENE, *American Historical Explanations—A Strategy for Grounded Enquiry* (Homewood, Illinois, 1973).

WITT, PETER-CHRISTIAN, *Die Finanzpolitik des Deutschen Reiches von 1903 bis 1913* (Lübeck and Hamburg, 1970).

WITTRAM, REINHARD, *Das Interesse an der Geschichte* (Göttingen, 1963).

WURM, FRANZ F., *Wirtschaft und Gesellschaft in Deutschland 1848–1948* (Opladen, 1969).

ZINNES, DINA A., NORTH, ROBERT C., and KOCH, HOWARD E. Jr., "Capability, Threat, and the Outbreak of War", in *International Politics and Foreign Policy,* edited by James N. Rosenau (Glencoe, Ill., 1961).

ZMARZLIK, HANS-GÜNTER, "Der Sozialdarwinismus in Deutschland als geschichtliches Problem", *VZ,* XI (1963), pp. 246–275.

——, *Bethmann Hollweg als Reichskanzler 1909–1914* (Düsseldorf, 1957).

INDEX